the FLOWER FARMERS

Inspiration & Advice from Expert Growers

the FLOWER FARMERS

Debra Prinzing & Robin Avni

Foreword by Christina Stembel, Farmgirl Flowers

ABRAMS, NEW YORK

With love to our husbands,
Bruce Brooks & Marc Avni

Contents

FOREWORD
Christina Stembel, Farmgirl Flowers
8

INTRODUCTION
10

FLORAL FUTURES
Becky Feasby, Prairie Girl Flowers
266

Opposite: Katie Tolson of Seed-on-Hudson has installed fencing to protect dahlias and other crops from the resident deer population, a constant pressure for area gardeners.

Foreword

It was just about a year ago that I was sitting in Debra Prinzing's backyard, the last of the day's sunlight winding its way through her (you may have already guessed, given the nature of this book, *incredible*) garden. The garden roses were in full bloom, and the cosmos had begun to bow their heads under the weight of their unfurling petals, as she shared the vision that she and her coauthor, Robin Avni, had for *this* very book that you're holding.

I've never had the chance to follow two authors as closely through the process of completing a project like this. And, I have to say, the enjoyment of having a front-row seat hasn't lessened but has somehow *grown* as I've watched them transform an idea into pages full of the stories of twenty-nine growers that feel as real, as buzzing with the sound of hurried bees, as they did that day in Debra's garden. I am so excited for you to enjoy the culmination of all of Robin's and Debra's work through the story you now hold in your hands: *The Flower Farmers.*

My own story—the story of Farmgirl Flowers—is decidedly less picturesque than what you will find here. There was no grandmother's cutting garden or bucolic farmhouse from which the business was born. It was, instead, a second-floor walk-up apartment on Van Ness Avenue in San Francisco where Farmgirl started and grew for its first two(ish) years of life.

After deciding I wanted to start my own business back in 2010, squarely amid the increasing fascination that we all had with online videos, I taught myself how to design the first Farmgirl bouquets the same way we were indulging our nostalgia with commercials from our childhood or learning to knit and purl: YouTube. Unconventional? Yes. But different was the plan from day one.

In an online market that was flooded with thousands of options that, in my opinion, always underdelivered on the promise their online photos had made, I started Farmgirl with a radically reduced lineup. Customers could buy just *one* daily arrangement, wrapped in burlap and filled with the best of the best I could source from the growers at the San Francisco Flower Market. But I didn't stop there.

My goal early on was to make sure there was at least one flower in every Farmgirl bouquet that the recipient had never seen before. With botanicals such as ornamental kale grown in Half Moon Bay, wild scabiosa that I'm 99 percent sure was picked from the side of Highway 1, and cymbidium orchids from the central coast, I created the signature mix of flowers and foliage that you'd never find growing side by side, the design vibe that Farmgirl is still known for today.

The business has come a long way since that second-floor walk-up where I was hydrating myrtle and eucalyptus in my bathtub and rigging makeshift coolers in the bay window with blackout curtains. But one thing that hasn't changed are the specialty cut flowers we're still using in our bouquets today, none of which would be possible without the equally special small and medium-size farms they come from—and the growers behind them. Romantic garden roses from a multigeneration farm in Salinas, California, or novelty daffodils from up in the Willamette Valley are part of the big differences that, to this day, make our bouquets feel special and our recipients feel loved, celebrated, and seen.

These flowers represent some of the important details that our customers have come to know and love Farmgirl for, but ones that, until this book, they may not have thought much about—beyond the bouquet they've admired. Creating connections between friends and loved ones has been our bread and butter for over a decade, and I am so excited for *The Flower Farmers* to create those same connections, but between the people who love these flowers and the incredible people who grow them.

Christina Stembel
Founder & CEO, Farmgirl Flowers
Oakland, California

Introduction

We usually meet the flowers first; then we consider the farmer whose hands grew those blooms.

What we know begins with the crops they grow; the uncommon, wistfully romantic botanicals that most of us first encounter at the farmers' market, or possibly at a roadside farm stand or you-pick field.

During the past several decades, we've witnessed the rising celebrity of the farmer and floral influencers. This phenomenon began with farm-to-table dining, the Slow Food movement, organic gardening, and other culinary trends and soon inspired a fascination with flower farming. When we know the farmer and learn about their journey to the land, the farming lifestyle is even more alluring.

The dirt welcomes everyone. Growing a patch of flowers (or food) is filled with possibility. You may have (or borrow use of) a small portion of land; you may possess a raised bed or a few pots on a patio or balcony, but all you need to add is sunshine, water, and a dose of sweat equity. A packet of sunflower seeds costs less than five dollars and will yield an abundance of good cheer when their tall stems soar above your head and their golden petals unfurl in perfect symmetry.

As journalists and consumer trend researchers, we've not only tracked the growth of floral entrepreneurship, but also the demographic rise of flower lovers who we call "farm adjacent." These are people who desire to know the "how, where, and who" behind the seasonal bouquets and bunches of flowers we enjoy.

Like a brilliant ribbon of orange, one row of poppies stretches across a cover-cropped field at 3 Porch Farm in Comer, Georgia. The quirky addition happened when Steve and Mandy O'Shea found themselves with more plants than what fit in their greenhouses, so they planted the extra poppies for the benefit of pollinators.

Additionally, we want our purchases and choices to feel meaningful; we want to connect with nature and experience the mystery of plants. Gardeners, florists, and nature lovers may not farm themselves, but they yearn to integrate the character and attributes of a flower farm into their backyards.

Modern-day flower lovers are most likely a few generations removed from their ancestors' agricultural-based lives. We often romanticize the idea of self-sufficient farming. Growing flowers has become a top activity among gardeners, second only to growing their own tomato or patch of basil. Notably, this includes more men than ever and more millennials than ever. Research about the physical and mental health benefits of growing and tending to plants has propelled even more folks to pick up a trowel and plant a garden.

For many of the flower farmers profiled in these pages, the first chapter of their story also began with a few seed packets, or a seedling that a friend or family member dug up and shared, or their response to a vacant parcel of land calling out for cultivation. As individuals, couples, multigenerational families, and friends who cofarm, they have come together to build floral enterprises that not only provide a livelihood, but also offer a rewarding lifestyle that was once viewed as unconventional. But now, not so much. It's the substance that dreams are made of.

It's no surprise to learn that as storytellers, we had thousands of potential flower farmers to consider when developing this book. Our shared goal was to introduce and profile farmers whose stories are uniquely inspiring, whose climatic and geographic conditions are relatable to a wide range of gardeners across the North American continent, and who were willing to impart their wisdom and expertise. They openly share the beauty and grit of their farm through photography while our interviews with each reveal the truths, challenges, and hard work required of flower farmers—and yes, the glorious sense of achievement experienced when a desired crop flourishes. Their path to the land and cultivation of a farm-based enterprise may instigate your desire to embrace a life in flowers, as well.

If you feel the pull and potential promise of growing your own bouquet, it's time to explore the many routes to your floral lifestyle. The methods and practices may vary, but the insights from twenty-nine farms profiled in *The Flower Farmers* will get you started. Adopt their techniques and tips and plant at least one of the featured botanicals that accompany their stories.

We've embraced this lifestyle ourselves, so take it from two converts. There's nothing more satisfying, more deeply rewarding, than enjoying flowers throughout the seasons, especially the ones you can grow yourself.

Opposite: Lisianthus plants at Six Dutchess Farm grow on stems that are four-to-five-feet tall with three to five open blooms. The remaining buds add charming texture and detailed interest, but they will not open once cut.

the FLOWER FARMERS

East / Northeast

Jennifer Kouvant & Hans Li
SIX DUTCHESS FARM

Six open windows flanked the stable, each framing a stately horse that peered right at him. That's the precise moment when Hans Li decided to name his new country getaway Six Dutchess Farm.

He was drawn to the Hudson Valley horse farm (in New York's Dutchess County) on a quest to escape Manhattan, and for years it was a weekend destination while Hans continued working as an architectural designer. The twelve-acre property had a house originally built in 1869, with the more contemporary additions of stable and outbuildings. Hans restored the home, added a chef's kitchen, and built beds for an edible garden. For more than ten years, the farm boarded horses.

Two decades later, Six Dutchess Farm is a cottage business producing fiber, food, and flowers, run by Hans and his wife, Jennifer Kouvant, a former international humanitarian worker and United Nations officer. The couple say there was a gradual, multiyear transition from being weekenders who owned a boutique horse farm to full-time stewards of a specialty cut flower farm, fruit orchards, apiaries, and a flock of gentle Gotland sheep.

They began treating their New York City apartment as the remote outpost, making the seventy-mile drive from Hudson Valley to deliver Six Dutchess Farm's community-supported agriculture (CSA) subscriptions of flowers, berries, fresh eggs, and honey to friends in the city. "We just started growing more and experimenting with different crops, which made it much harder to leave, as we planted and cared for nature," Jennifer says. Eventually, the couple packed up decades of belongings and made the permanent move to the farm.

To date, the two have managed the farm with only a grounds crew. "Hans is very much the builder and he handles anything to do with mechanics and developing spaces," Jennifer says. "So much of the beautiful documentation of our farm, the photography, the videos—that's Hans's work. Then, there are the animals, especially in the wintertime, when he takes care of the sheep. We manage the bees together and I do more of the growing, the harvest, developing new clients, and putting the educational classes together." They introduced on-farm events recently, thanks to a decision to transform a stable into a classroom for floral and cooking workshops.

A seasonal rhythm of growth, harvest, and rest frames life at Six Dutchess Farm. Yet in the past few seasons, the flower farming cycle has rapidly expanded. Cut flower production has

Opposite: Jennifer Kouvant and Hans Li bring their shared passion for the land and their personal histories to Six Dutchess Farm. A native of New York City, Jennifer spent more than a decade in international humanitarian work prior to meeting and marrying Hans Li in 2007. A native of Hong Kong, Hans was raised in Germany and educated from his teenage years in the United States.

Above from top: The front of Jennifer and Hans's residence was designed to replicate the facade of the original 1869 farmhouse, providing views of the gardens and pond. Young orchard trees dot the grounds in the foreground, where the deciduous woods provide an important windbreak to protect cut flowers. *Opposite*: Rows of summer annuals and perennials fill the fields at Six Dutchess Farm. The field crops include dahlia, eucalyptus, China aster, snapdragon, yarrow, nigella, and phlox. Each year, Jennifer and Hans trial a few new flowers, including in recent seasons, bearded iris, campanula, and Iceland poppy.

more than doubled, encouraged by positive responses at local farmers' markets and an increasing wholesale base of wedding and event florists.

The floral season begins with early bulb crops, including winter tulips grown inside in crates to cheat the season and satisfy bloom-hungry customers. April and May produce fragrant narcissus, field tulips, ranunculus, and anemones, followed by the summer crops: lisianthus and many companion annuals that appear in mixed bouquets, such as rudbeckia, China asters, cosmos, and snapdragons. Late-summer dahlias fill out the year until the first frost. Spring, summer, and fall phases yield plenty of stems to supply customers in the Hudson Valley and beyond with floral share subscriptions.

Jennifer and Hans encourage subscribers to pick up weekly shares at the market stall or their farm stand. "Farmers' markets remind us why we farm," Jennifer says. "We love the connection with our customers, and that means we have to get off of the farm and meet the people we want to sell to." That personal connection is critical to the future of small farming, she believes. "We know that what we sell is more expensive than (flowers at) big-box stores or bodegas. Yet when people know you and see how you grow, and appreciate the quality and longevity of your flowers, they're much more likely to buy from a small farm like ours."

Jennifer and Hans sell both "straight bunches" and designer-market bouquets. While more labor-intensive to make, "there is no getting around the fact that when we bring mixed bunches, they sell really well," Jennifer acknowledges. "We try to bring things to market that we know nobody else has, and we want our flowers to start a conversation. We also trial flowers at the market before growing them in larger quantities. This year, we trialed campanula and jumbo Icelandic poppies and the response was insane. People crossed the market to see the poppies, and said, 'Oh, my God, what is this? We've never seen these kinds of flowers!'"

That is the experience of wonderment and curiosity they want to give their community, Hans adds. "One of the greatest rewards for me is watching how happy Jennifer is to talk with people at the farmers' market. We're not just selling flowers; we're selling a story and sharing stories, which means our world becomes much greater because of these human connections."

Opposite, clockwise from top left: Sheep are beneficial to the small farm in so many ways, say Hans and Jennifer. "In their gentle, calming wanderings, they fertilize the soil and help redistribute carbon back to the land through rotational grazing practices." The Six Dutchess Farm flock is used exclusively for fiber production and soil restoration. The 17,000-square-foot barn was built by a previous owner, originally with an indoor riding arena and stalls to house eight horses. Six Dutchess Farm's 100 percent pure raw honey is hand harvested. "As a small family farm, we rely on honey sales to fund our apiary program. What we earn in sales, we put back into the bees—providing a safe foraging space, free of chemical pesticides and synthetic fertilizers," Jennifer and Hans explain.

Previous spread: Jennifer tends to field plantings of lisianthus and veronica. The farm's high-quality lisianthus have opened doors to serve the florist market through a wholesale program. "We've developed some of our most loyal florist buyers and event florists, who assumed we'd been growing lizzies for many years," Jennifer says. *Opposite*: Buckets and bunches of lisianthus become the botanical billboard for Six Dutchess Farm's stall at a local Hudson Valley farmers' market. Hans jokes that people driving past the market slam on their brakes when they see the blooms he and Jennifer have on display. *Above*: The high tunnels provide an ideal microclimate for Six Dutchess Farm's prolific lisianthus crops. The 50-foot-long tunnels accommodate lisianthus starts, organized by variety. The side panels and doorways can be rolled up to regulate temperature and ensure good air circulation, and the broad central walkway ensures that Jennifer and Hans can navigate the rows.

LISIANTHUS

Eustoma russellianum, also known
as *Eustoma grandiflorum*
(other common names, Texas bluebell and prairie gentian)

24″–36″
Full Sun
Prefers moist, loamy soil
Native perennial, grown as an annual

FAVORITE VARIETIES

Lisianthus 'Advantage', 'Arena', 'Celeb', 'Corelli', 'Croma',
'Falda', 'Grace', 'Megalo', 'Sabrina', and 'Voyage'

Below: The lisianthus form entices flower farmers, florists, and flower lovers alike. The popular summer flower, a hybrid of a North American native perennial that was originally a prairie wildflower nicknamed Texas bluebell, is now a luxury wedding and event bloom favored by florists.

The name *Eustoma*, from the Greek *eu* ("good") and *stoma* ("mouth"), refers to the bloom's large-throated opening, a feature that rivals the rose for its size and beauty in floral design. The extremely showy flower is a perennial native to the moist places (streams, rivers) of west-central North America, but specialty cut flower growers treat lisianthus as annuals. With succulent-like, blue-gray foliage and tall stems that bear single and double blooms, lisianthus produces a wide range of hues. "From deep blues to blushes, pinks, peaches and apricots, yellows, greens, and all of our favorite lavenders, the subtleties and variations are endless," Jennifer notes.

Wild populations of the native Texas bluebell are threatened, but hybrids developed for the floral trade are only gaining in visibility and popularity among growers and their customers, including wedding and event designers eager for a versatile and long-lasting focal flower.

Six Dutchess Farm considers lisianthus (often referred to by the nickname "lizzie" or "lizzies") one of its signature flowers, devoting three 50-foot-long high tunnels to the production of dozens of varieties and colors. Their foray into the high-value summer crop followed a year when the dahlias in Six Dutchess Farm's first high tunnel overheated and failed. "I was terrified of growing anything in the high tunnel after the dahlia fiasco, but I heard lisianthus do well in that type of covered, hot environment," Jennifer says. She credits much of the season's success to careful soil preparation and ideal conditions of heat and air flow, but also to the attention she devoted to checking for root rot and other fungal disease. "It is the ideal 'nervous mom' flower. We find it imperative to monitor lisianthus daily and look for signs of rotting, which requires quick removal to stop the spread. Plant plugs require root soaking in biofungicides before planting. If you can get past these impediments, you are on the right path to a magical experience."

Lisianthus can be grown from seed, but most flower farmers opt to order plugs (small, rooted plant starts) from trusted cut flower suppliers. Growing lisianthus from plugs provides a significant shortcut, saving months of otherwise slow seed germination and indoor seeding space, often in short supply on a small farm.

When asked, Jennifer and Hans say they favor all lavender varieties of lisianthus. "We try and look at the market and see what varieties event florists are asking for, what market customers love, and also what other farms may not grow. We look at our sales numbers and talk with our best customers on the wholesale side to get a sense of their wish lists. But honestly, if lisianthus never sells we would still grow it because it's so beautiful," Jennifer says.

Most growers harvest other annuals and perennials when they are in bud, in order to extend the flowers' longevity. "The lisianthus is one of the few flowers for which we do the opposite," Jennifer notes. "We usually wait until there are three or four open flowers before we cut the stem, because those buds won't open once harvested."

"Lisianthus is the ultimate summer flower," Jennifer notes. "We've been rewarded with thousands upon thousands of frilly, multicolored blooms that keep for up to three weeks in the cooler and vase. They are the most majestic, elegant, giving flowers we have ever encountered and they are just perfect for Six Dutchess Farm."

WHEN TO PLANT
At Six Dutchess Farm, lisianthus plugs are planted in early to mid-April while nights are still cool.

WHERE TO BUY
Plugs:
  Farmer Bailey (Gro 'n Sell), farmerbailey.com
Seeds: Six Dutchess Farm does not grow lisianthus from seed, due to its slow seed germination and their limited temperature-controlled space, but there are numerous sources for lisianthus seeds. Mail-order sources:
  Johnny's Selected Seeds (ships to United States and Canada), johnnyseeds.com

HOW TO WATER
Once plugs are planted, they should be watered thoroughly (by an overhead method), daily for 2–3 days until established. Once established, the plants are watered daily until the soil is moist but not overly wet. Some growers saturate the soil for several hours and then don't water again until the soil is dry. Jennifer notes that lisianthus can withstand dry conditions and are susceptible to disease if excessively wet.

WHEN TO HARVEST
In the northeast United States, where Six Dutchess Farm is based, lisianthus are ready for harvest in summer, with bloom time from July through September. (Some growers enjoy a second bloom flush from September through November, usually with high tunnel or greenhouse conditions.) Harvest when multiple flowers are in full bloom. Buds do not tend to open after harvest.

Leon and Carol Carrier & Leon (Lee) Carrier III
PLANT MASTERS

The Carrier family has been growing cut flowers and plants for more than forty years, raising their three children with a love for flowers, and keeping the business in the family as it transitions into the hands of the next generation.

Plant Masters, the specialty cut flower farm owned by Leon and Carol Carrier, is based in Laytonsville, Maryland, twenty miles north of the nation's capital. They are high school sweethearts who came to flower farming from ornamental horticulture (Leon) and the fashion industry (Carol). Those talents are melded into a family-owned floral enterprise that supplies numerous farmers' markets in Maryland and the District of Columbia with an abundance of bouquets and blooms.

Leon recalls the moment he decided to add cut flowers to his nursery and bedding-plant business. He was a horticulture student at the University of Maryland and sold his plants at a weekend farmers' market. "Right next to me, there was a farmer who brought something like fifty buckets of lilac blooms when they were in season. And I watched the frenzy as customers went crazy for those flowers. I thought, 'I want that,' because my pots of cactus plants weren't creating a craze like the lilacs."

As a grower, Leon also realized that farmers' market shoppers purchased plants every few months, but they often purchased flowers each week.

Leon and Carol found their land in the 1980s, and soon, the few acres surrounding the family house were not enough to contain the explosion of field crops and greenhouses they had installed there. Leon approached several neighbors with a land-barter proposal, and soon established satellite parcels across four other gardens. The scheme added up to four acres and resembled more of a patchwork quilt than a vast agricultural operation.

"It's like an arboretum here," Leon acknowledges of the home farm. "I love plants. I love unusual plants. As you can imagine, having lived and farmed on this same property for so many years, we have amazing botanical diversity." The Carriers embraced flower farming at a time when specialty cut flowers were mostly viewed as an add-on crop at a vegetable farm. Today, Plant Masters is known for its year-round selection of floral design elements and more than one hundred plant varieties, beginning with woody ornamental branches and early flowering bulbs in winter; hellebores, peonies, and perennials in spring; hydrangeas, sunflowers, dahlias, and numerous annual blooms during the summer; and

Opposite: Lee (left) joins his parents, Leon and Carol, on a tour through the greenhouse, one of several original structures installed on their home property in Laytonsville, Maryland.

PLANTMASTERSFLOWERS.COM | @PLANTMASTERSFLOWERS

heirloom mums, winter greenery, winterberry branches, dried flowers, and forced bulbs like paperwhites and amaryllis by the year's end.

"We know our flowers are special, but we also know that people can find flowers in many other places," Carol says. "We do a lot of education, and most of the people who buy from us really want our flowers. They seek us out and prize what we grow." Recently, Plant Masters helped establish the Chesapeake Flower Exchange, a collective of ten Maryland farms that sells direct to florists. This adds another year-round sales channel for their flowers, as the collective increases Plant Masters' exposure to a broader audience of floral professionals.

While his two sisters have established themselves in non-farming professions, Leon (Lee) Carrier III, the eldest child (who was just six years old when Plant Masters began), is now Carol and Leon's business partner. "Growing up, I would go to markets with them, to the greenhouses to check out new plants, and even into the woods with my Dad to harvest wild bittersweet," Lee recalls. "I was exposed to farming at an early age."

In recent years, Plant Masters has expanded beyond the original home property to a new five-acre farm. Relocating several high tunnels and shifting other operations allows them to do things better, Leon explains. "We tried to design better planting layouts, and we utilize the barn, which means we can load flowers direct from the cooler into the truck—outside of the rain." The land has plenty of acreage for rows of annual flowers, but it also accommodates more perennials including peonies and shrubs like lilacs, quince, and hydrangeas. Leon still starts most of the seeds, but he has begun to document the seasonal planting schedule that has (up until now) been done from memory. "I'm thinking of giving him a waterproof notebook so he can write down the seed varieties and dates when everything gets planted," Lee says.

With two generations now operating Plant Masters, it's impressive that the family adheres to one important annual tradition. "From the very beginning, we take off two weeks each year," Carol says. "The entire family goes, and that means our employees have to step up and run the show." They value this mid-season break. "We work like crazy and get all the summer annuals planted; then we head to the beach."

Reflecting on their more than four decades of flower farming, Leon marvels at the choice he made to specialize in flower farming rather than cactus-growing. "We grow flowers, but we sell happiness," he proclaims. "You can imagine all of those years we've brought flowers to farmers' markets. That's a lot of happiness."

Opposite: Leon takes a break during winterberry harvest to rest on a cart and tie a bunch of stems. *Above*: Barn dogs Goldie and Bear protect the flower fields from deer damage. As Carol puts it: "Everyone has to earn their keep!"

WINTERBERRY

Ilex verticillata cultivars

12′ tall × 12′ wide
Full Sun
Prefers wet or moist soil
Woody shrub

FAVORITE VARIETIES
Ilex verticillata 'Winter Gold', 'Winter Red'

Below: Ilex verticillata 'Winter Red'.

Winterberry is a high-value specialty crop that has a short but potentially lucrative season for flower farmers. The shrubs are multistemmed and produce straight branches perfect for cutting. Rather than bearing the prickly leaves of its English holly relative, *Ilex aquifolium*, winterberry produces small, smooth leaves and glossy orange or red berries in little clusters along its branches. Often, leaves are still left attached to the branches, but most growers and designers prefer to remove them before winterberry is used in floral arrangements.

The plants are native to the eastern North America and grow into large shrubs. Plant Masters has hundreds of winterberry shrubs in several varieties. Leon credits fourteen-year-old Lee for helping him establish it as one of their best-selling crops. "I ordered one hundred 'Winter Red' plants—they were two-gallon plants, so he had to dig some pretty big holes," he jokes. "But when you're that age, you have more energy than your dad."

After the success of the first planting, Leon ordered three hundred winterberry plugs from a commercial nursery. "I talked to a couple of neighbors and got permission to plant in their culverts. These are trenches that direct the runoff during rainstorms, which is perfect for the winterberry shrubs—because they like wet feet."

The two most typical berry colors—orange and red—align perfectly with fall and winter holiday seasons. "We start cutting orange winterberry in September because that leads into fall floral

Above: Wearing her "bracelet" of rubber bands for tying bunches, Carol gathers the 'Winter Gold' cultivar, *Ilex verticillata*.

design—Halloween and Thanksgiving," Leon explains. After Thanksgiving, sales of red-fruiting winterberry quickly replace the orange-berry branches. "The good thing about this type of *Ilex* is that you can use it indoors, in a foyer display, or shorter in centerpieces. And a lot of our customers stick branches in their outdoor containers for the season," he adds.

WHEN TO PLANT

Plant winterberry shrubs in fall or spring, spacing them 4' to 6' apart. The plant is dioecious, with separate male and female plants, so consult with a nursery to make sure you have the proper ratio to ensure berry production. Only female varieties are harvested, and not all male plants pollinate all female ones.

WHERE TO BUY

Most specialty nurseries and garden centers supply winterberry plants or can special-order plants for you. Mail-order sources:
  Bluestone Perennials, bluestoneperennials.com
  Spring Hill Nurseries, springhillnursery.com
  White Flower Farm, whiteflowerfarm.com

HOW TO WATER

These shrubs take several years to establish and begin berry production, so they will need regular water while maturing, especially throughout dry seasons.

WHEN TO HARVEST

Harvest branches beginning in mid-fall. The berries do not deepen in color once branches are cut, so select branches with nearly ripe berries before cutting. Plant Masters cuts winterberry at various lengths to suit their customers' needs—with bunches that include 12- to 14-inch-long branches, 24-inch-long branches, and up to 5-foot-long branches for large wedding and event installations.

Abby & Derek Matson
DIDDLE & ZEN

When Abby Matson tells the story of how she and her husband, Derek Matson, found a historic Vermont farm, purchased it, and moved across the country from Denver in the course of just a few months, it sounds like a dream.

To find their twenty-eight-acre farm in Panton, Vermont, and its 1805 stone farmhouse, Abby leveraged her skills as a real estate agent to hunt online. The couple wanted to live within forty minutes of any airport, making it easy for Derek to travel for his job in multifamily housing. "We were looking in different areas of New England, and Vermont was the last state that entered our search," Abby says. "But once I realized there was an airport in Burlington, our house was one of the first ones that popped up. It checked all the boxes, and I seriously thought it was too good to be true." She loved the old farmhouse and was charmed by bucolic images of the big red dairy barn and its outbuildings, all of which promised an antidote to the burnout she felt.

After working in real estate for a dozen years, Abby knew she was removed from her desire to live a creative life, and she wanted to change things. "Also, Derek and I both grew up in rural areas, so we always had this plan to eventually own some land. I like being physical and I like the kind of work where you see the results at the end of the day, not necessarily having to be in front of a computer all the time. Flowers were just a serendipitous answer." Curiosity about flower farming led Abby to take an online farming course, which accelerated the transition to Vermont. "We did everything in six months: the class, the move, everything. I even ordered seeds and flower plugs before we closed on the house. I was desperate to have flowers that first year," she recalls.

Today, their dream of a rural lifestyle is supported by the perennials, annuals, and bulb flowers that they grow at Diddle & Zen. The farm-based enterprise offers wedding florals, operates a farm stand and retail flower shop, and hosts farm tours.

Diddle & Zen is a tribute to two former pets, Weimaraners whose nicknames were combined to create their farm's name. "Now we have Gunnie and Ghost," Abby says of their current Weimaraner farm dogs.

With crop-planning guidance from the farming course, Abby planned her initial 45′ × 100′ field in the spring. "I remember standing in the little hobby greenhouse here, looking at the plugs

Opposite: Abby Matson of Diddle & Zen is a Vermont flower farmer and florist. She and her husband, Derek Matson, have created a diverse agricultural business compatible with their desire to have a country lifestyle. Abby shows off a long-sleeve Diddle & Zen graphic T-shirt, also used for brand marketing.

DIDDLEANDZEN.COM | @DIDDLEANDZEN

and thinking, 'I hope you don't die.'" She chuckles. "They were all so little!" But her seedlings rooted, and she recalls, "everything was a miracle to me—every moment."

Abby soon learned about the character of their land's Addison County clay. "It is not nice," she remarks. "The native grass here has roots that you just keep pulling and pulling and pulling. We still deal with it a lot, but we amend each year with a fresh layer of compost before each planting. We till a tiny bit, but just to turn in our cover crop and to loosen the top of the soil."

Raised beds in some areas provide better cultural conditions for plants like anemones, ranunculus, tulips, and dahlias; in other areas, they laid landscape cloth to suppress more grass over the winter. "The method gave us a whole new field and a better start for the next year," she explains. They have since erected a 30′ × 60′ heated greenhouse for early season crops and have added a walk-in cooler inside the barn, where Abby and her seasonal design assistants produce wedding florals.

Abby credits getting involved in the community with much of her success in finding markets for Diddle & Zen's flowers. Their farm faces Jersey Street, which is on the route to the Crown Point Bridge, one of the few southern ways to cross Lake Champlain into New York State. "We also get a lot of the seasonal crowd going to and from the Basin Harbor Club."

Owners of the resort and boating club have tapped Abby to provide flowers for the lobby and dining room. There's also a Diddle & Zen floral add-on option for guests who choose to order arrangements for their hotel rooms.

During flower season, shoppers visit Diddle & Zen's farm stand, a 9′ × 14′ shed situated near the road and open for business mid-April until October. The honor system works well for customers who purchase bunches or market bouquets; they use the QR code to pay digitally or pop cash or a check in the old-fashioned cash box. "We have paper sleeves and rubber bands out there; sometimes I'll take empty spaghetti jars for people who want to travel with their flowers in water," Abby adds.

The farm itself isn't open to the public, but customers kept asking to visit. This interest led to the Sunset Farm Tours, held July through September. "We usually plan for two dates each month and allow up to twenty people per event, just to keep it manageable. Each guest receives a harvest bucket. I give them a tour of the fields and some instruction on how to harvest different flowers. Then we set them loose with their snips and buckets." After they finish, Abby invites the guests to place their flowers in the cooler to help hydrate the stems, and they join the group at a big dining table on the lawn to enjoy wine, a charcuterie board, and desserts at sunset.

Opposite, clockwise from top left: A raised bed planted with spring-blooming grape hyacinth bulbs. Guests who arrive for Diddle & Zen's Sunset Tour are invited to follow Abby into the flower fields to learn about growing a flower garden while they fill their buckets with just-picked stems.
Following spread: The Sunset Farm Tour concludes with refreshments on the lawn, including beverages and a charcuterie service crafted by local chefs. Alfresco-style events take place on the lawn, where seating and tables are placed between the Matson's home and the flower farm.

Field-grown crops flourish near Diddle &
Zen's pair of high tunnels. The doors
can open, and the sides can be raised to
adjust temperature and air circulation,
depending on weather changes.

Abby and Derek recently purchased a twenty-year-old flower shop in Vergennes, a neighboring town just six miles from the farm. Not surprisingly, the acquisition came with established customers near and far. "When you're in a small area like this, the local flower shop is kind of an institution—so many people have considered it their shop for prom flowers, weddings, funerals," she says. "It feels like an important role to take on and have the goodwill of the community." Abby and her team reorganized the space to create a gift and home-goods area and a floral production area that's visible to customers who like to see how their flower orders come together.

Abby acknowledges that she's working to balance flower farming demands with her floral design work, in addition to running two farm-and-town locations. She tells herself that she doesn't have to grow every flower she wants to use for wedding designs, for example. "There are so many other great local farms, so I can also source from them. But there's nothing like the convenience of my process—I love to walk around the farm and see what I've grown while creating a bouquet in my mind as I harvest. I would miss out on that experience if I didn't have the farm."

At left from top: The garden shed turned farm stand greets passersby who stop at Diddle & Zen to pick up bouquets for the weekend. French flower buckets arranged by variety and color are part of the bouquet bar inside the Diddle & Zen farm stand, where customers shop on the honor system. *Opposite*: After acquiring a Vergennes, Vermont, floral studio, Abby and Derek relocated the shop to Main Street in a bright, cheerful space where passersby are lured through the front door to see Diddle & Zen's flowers.

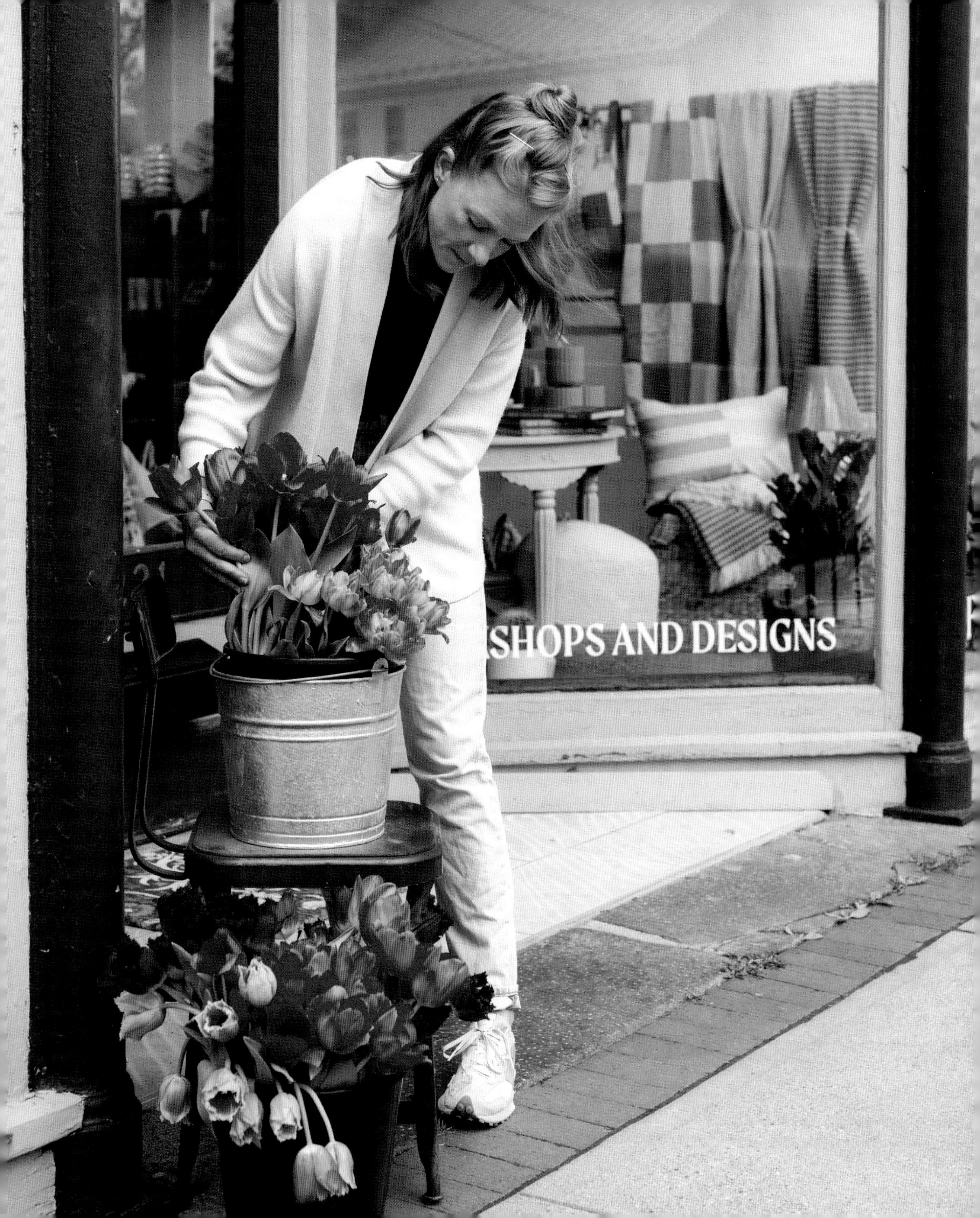
SHOPS AND DESIGNS

GOOSENECK LOOSESTRIFE

Lysimachia clethroides

36"–40"
Full to Part Shade
Prefers moist soil; will tolerate dry conditions in shade,
    but plants will not flourish; vigorous spreader
Perennial

FAVORITE VARIETY

Lysimachia clethroides 'Lady Jane'

Below: Gooseneck loosestrife (*Lysimachia clethroides*), a favorite perennial that adds movement and texture to floral arrangements and to garden borders.

The nodding heads of *Lysimachia clethroides,* also called gooseneck loosestrife, display a sense of movement even when the wind is still. This is a hardy perennial with mainly upright stems that produce 4- to 5-inch-long pointed flowers that curve in the shape of a goose's neck. Arching spikes are covered in tiny star-shaped flowers; the dark green leaves are lance-shaped and grow horizontally.

The genus name honors King Lysimachus (361–281 BCE), Macedonian king of Thrace, who, legend has it, once tamed an ox with the plant. Native to parts of China, Japan, and Europe, gooseneck loosestrife is in Primulaceae, the primrose family.

It's a favorite cut flower for wedding designers and bouquet makers and a versatile plant all season long. Before it blooms in midsummer, the downy, serrated foliage is great for spring bouquets. At the peak of the season, the white blooms dance above and around companion flowers in every direction. "It can be a beautiful line flower in a bouquet, but it's not as stiff or bulky as snapdragon, for example," Abby says. "I love this flower when I need a delicate element to my designs."

Gooseneck loosestrife isn't just a special-occasion flower. "I definitely use it in market bouquets. It's so productive that I don't really have to hold back!"

Because this perennial spreads by robust rhizomes (underground stems), it can be aggressive in the

Above: The couple's two Weimaraner farm dogs are constant companions around the farm. Here, Gunnie supervises Abby's early spring planting efforts.

garden border or in boggy areas. Abby contains her plants by growing them in a 3′ × 14′ raised bed, which provides a defined boundary that prevents spreading. "I planted twenty-five plugs the first year and they put on a decent show. By the next year, the entire raised bed was full," she notes. She does not plant gooseneck loosestrife with other perennial flowers.

WHEN TO PLANT

Plant this perennial in the spring after the last frost. Gardeners can purchase potted *Lysimachia* plants from online nurseries and specialty garden centers. While some flower farmers start their crops from seed, Abby prefers to order prerooted plugs to save time and give her a jump-start on the growing season.

WHERE TO BUY

Retail nurseries:

  Breck's, brecks.com

  White Flower Farm, whiteflowerfarm.com

Plug sources:

  Farmer Bailey (Gro 'n Sell), farmerbailey.com

HOW TO WATER

Water to establish in the first season. In subsequent seasons, as gooseneck loosestrife prefers moist soil, water weekly throughout the growing season.

WHEN TO HARVEST

Cut when the flowers at the base of each spike are beginning to open. Reach deep down to the base of each stem to clip, ensuring you'll have 24″ or longer stems for floral arranging.

Marly Surena-Llorens
FENIMORE & RUTLAND

Marly Surena-Llorens was born and raised in the United States, but her Haitian mother's stories of tropical gardens filled with palms, crotons, and bougainvillea plants inspired her lifelong love of flowers. Yet, Marly says some of her most vivid floral impressions came from the BBC programs of her youth, when she watched period TV dramas in her family's apartment. "If you knew me as a child, you wouldn't be surprised by my love of cottage gardens, because I was very much into English literature and those British television shows. I read all the Brontë sisters, too. I don't know if it was just finding an escape or seeking the beauty of what I saw on television, but I wanted that for myself. Those memories have stayed with me forever and have really informed my floral designs," she recalls.

Today she gardens and grows cut flowers on two residential lots in Allentown, Pennsylvania, a college town located about one hour north of Philadelphia. Marly describes herself as a "farmer who designs," and with just a quarter of an acre, her land produces enough flowers for Fenimore & Rutland's seasonal bouquet subscriptions, wedding florals, and design workshops. "When I first purchased this house, it never occurred to me that I could build a business on my land," she explains. "It was always my intention to do something with flowers when I retired, but at some point, I realized, 'Why don't I just start?' Now, my flowers evoke whatever mood the customer wants to express, whether it's sorrow or loss, or beauty, or gift giving."

Marly has worked in corporate insurance for nearly three decades, but she wanted to find a creative outlet beyond her full-time career. She originally formed Fenimore & Rutland as a design studio to produce floral photography, stationery, and other custom-printed items. The business borrows its name from two tree-lined streets near her childhood home in Brooklyn. "At its core, I created Fenimore & Rutland with the intention of building community," Marly points out, noting that she works remotely with a team of colleagues around the country, which can feel isolating.

As the firstborn child of a first-generation immigrant family, it was expected that she would be a high achiever, earning undergraduate and graduate degrees and pursuing a professional career. "In the Haitian culture, there's a saying that translates as 'Home, school, and church.' That's the triad of what's important in your life. Education is emphasized highly; it's ingrained in the culture that achieving is very important."

Opposite: In her new studio, located in Bethlehem, Pennsylvania, a short distance from her neighborhood, Marly now has her own workspace. She rents a 100-square-foot area for production, design workshops, and use of a sizeable floral cooler from another wedding florist for whom she also freelances. The space allows her to connect with more customers and students in her community, while giving her some distance from where she lives and farms.

FENIMORERUTLAND.COM | @FENIMORE_RUTLAND

Rather than buying flowers for her photography sessions, Marly started a cutting garden to grow her own. "I didn't even know that flower farming was a thing, but I realized that growing my own flowers would be a less expensive way to photograph flowers for my stationery line," she explains. The garden quickly expanded and wooed her away from flower photography. She removed the lawn and began to amend the soil with healthy compost, building the garden's foundation. "For my first crop, I planted rows of double tulips. I wanted to experience the full life cycle during one growing season."

The backyard now contains four 60-foot-long rows of raised beds and several perennial flower sections. "I'm moving slowly towards having seventy-five percent perennials—peonies, hellebores, and specialty daffodils, which I treat as perennials. I also grow more shrubs for greenery—viburnum, spiraea, hydrangeas—and David Austin garden roses," she notes. These ingredients are the basis for seasonal floral subscriptions—spring, summer, and fall collections and a dedicated dahlia collection available in September and October. The business has grown through word of mouth and through social media. "Hyperlocal selling has helped to increase my customer base within a ten-mile radius, which allows me to supply my community," she adds.

During the growing season (spring through fall), this mother of two spends most of her evenings and weekends immersed in her floral business. "I've given up the idea of balance," she confides with a laugh. Marly begins each day early, spending a few hours harvesting, processing, and photographing flower varieties before logging onto her computer for her day job. "I cut my flowers at their prime and quickly get them into the cooler. I also take note of the quantities and varieties to update availabilities for my wholesale buyers." After work, she preps for orders or transplants seedlings. Yes, this means regular sixteen-hour days. "It's a real hustle and, to be honest, it's not a perfect work-life balance, but it doesn't always feel like work when I'm out in my fields," she confides.

Previous spread: During flower season, Marly begins and ends her days in the flower beds, where she harvests in the early morning and packs orders after hours. As a flower farmer who designs, Marly has transformed her residential garden outside of Philadelphia into a small-scale flower farm that produces perennials, annuals, and flowering bulb crops—the ingredients for subscription bouquets and small wedding orders. *Clockwise from top left*: Dahlias and sunflowers, seen here at the height of summer, evoke English cottage gardens. A charming single dahlia is an excellent addition to the cutting garden, but also, due to Marly's sustainable growing practices, is safe for insects to pollinate. Marly's love of flowers began during her childhood. As an adult, she has built a life around flowers, one that provides income but, more importantly, creative fulfillment.

FOXGLOVE

Digitalis ferruginea, D. lanata, D. obscura, D. purpurea cultivars and hybrids

36"
Full Sun to Part Shade
Tender perennial or biennial

FAVORITE VARIETIES
Digitalis purpurea 'Dalmatian Peach',
    'Camelot Rose'

A classic cottage garden perennial, the foxglove grows as a beautiful spire, with its bloom stalk that towers above a low clump of leaves at the plant's base. The common garden foxglove, *Digitalis purpurea*, readily spreads and is often mistaken for a North American native plant, which it isn't. The name comes from the Latin word for finger *(digit)*, which is fitting, as the tubular blooms appear to be the perfect spot to tuck a fingertip inside. The flowers are popular with hummingbirds, frequently seen feeding on the nectar, and the little spots on each bell-shaped bloom are thought to guide bees to the pollen.

Foxgloves readily reseed as biennial plants; most produce seedlings one year and bloom the following year. There are some cultivars, such as *Digitalis purpurea* 'Dalmatian Peach', that flower the first year.

The plant's soft, spiked flowers stand tall in the back of the garden bed and are usually ignored by deer and rabbits. Foxgloves are celebrated by florists for the role they play as a line flower and dramatic design element. All parts of the *Digitalis* species contain poison, from roots to bloom.

Below: Foxgloves are the iconic cottage spring flower for the garden or vase. This stand of foxgloves illustrates the diversity of height of the flower spikes and the varied colors of the bell-shaped blooms.

WHEN TO PLANT

Start seed indoors in trays 10 to 12 weeks before the last frost; transplant out after all danger of frost has passed. Seeds are very small; bottom-watering is recommended until plants emerge.

WHERE TO BUY

Foxglove plants can often be found at nurseries and specialty garden centers in the annual or cottage garden section. Mail-order sources:

American Meadows, americanmeadows.com
Bluestone Perennials, bluestoneperennials.com
White Flower Farm, whiteflowerfarm.com

Many reputable seed providers offer a range of foxglove seeds, including:

Johnny's Seeds, johnnyseeds.com
Select Seeds, selectseeds.com

HOW TO WATER

Most plants need spring moisture before they bloom. Keep the soil moist but not soaked. Avoid overhead watering, which can encourage fungal disease. *D. ferruginea* handles dry soil well.

WHEN TO HARVEST

Harvest when just a few of the lower flowers on each stem are open and before the bees pollinate the flowers. Expect a vase life of 6 to 8 days.

At left from top: *Digitalis purpurea* 'Pink Gin', a second year–flowering cultivar that produces delicate, shell-pink bells with lightly freckled throats. *Digitalis lanata* 'Café Crème', a second year–flowering foxglove that produces petite pearl-gray blooms with brown-and-gold details. The colors blend together to create a mocha-cream palette, giving this beauty its delicious name.

Katie Tolson
SEED-ON-HUDSON

An artistic sensibility has guided Katie Tolson to create a life of plants, seeds, and flowers. Trained as an art appraiser, Katie has brought her curation skills to nature at Seed-on-Hudson, her home-based plant nursery and flower farm in Hastings-on-Hudson, ten miles north of Manhattan.

Her business name is a nod to the "on Hudson" river towns that extend north from the Bronx along the east side of the Hudson River. The motif continues to Seed-on-Hudson's logo and branding, created by British illustrator and printmaker Alice Pattullo, featuring the color palette and typography of Metro North's transit signage and a drawing of Hastings-on-Hudson's historic water tower.

The village has a history of attracting creatives and ecologically minded residents like Katie, whose background, in addition to the study of art history, includes art appraisal and a career in antiques and decorative arts. Initially, the art world brought Katie; her British husband, Dan Tolson; and their two young daughters to the New York City area. These days, plants are her medium, as Katie now specializes in growing fragrant and heirloom blooms using sustainable, pesticide-free practices.

"It's what I always should have been doing," she muses, reflecting on memories of favorite childhood summers spent on her great-uncle's Ohio farm. "I love the art world, but if, in my young adolescence, I had realized that I could make a living doing this, I would have grown plants instead."

While developing her less-than-half-acre garden, Katie took courses on herbalism and soil science at the New York Botanical Garden. Despite the property's limited size and challenging topography, she planted vegetables, flowers, fruits, herbs, and native plants, viewing the garden as a perfect place to combine a love of nature with her affinity for craft and design. She started Seed-on-Hudson as a plant nursery in spring 2020. "I tend to overseed, so I decided to offer extra plants to my neighbors— tomato and pepper plants for home gardens."

Katie's seed obsession grew, and in 2022 she brought plants and cut flowers to the local farmers' market, assisted by her eleven-year-old daughter, Imogen. When a local couple learned of Seed-on-Hudson's plant sales, they invited Katie to visit their nearby property, a historic home and garden with majestic views overlooking the Hudson River. That chance encounter led to Seed-on-Hudson planting a satellite farm where Katie

Opposite: Katie Tolson has immersed herself in a floral-filled life, which she sees as a natural extension of her childhood fascination with nature and her fine arts training.

SEEDONHUDSON.COM | @SEEDONHUDSON

now collaborates with the property owners. "They wanted to build a high tunnel and were looking for a partner to help them grow there year-round. It was literally like winning a Wonka kind of golden ticket!"

The couple installed a 1,200-square-foot high tunnel, and Katie contributed compost, seeds, plants, and sweat equity. Although it is unusual, the reciprocal arrangement has allowed Katie to expand what and how much she grows. She finds the tunnel ideal for raising early spring bulb crops like ranunculus and anemones, strawflowers in summer, and heirloom chrysanthemums in fall. Two additional planting areas are home to perennials, annuals, and dahlias, which prefer field conditions. "It's a beautiful place, with gorgeous amounts of sun. I feel so lucky just going there every day," she notes. "My friends are incredibly generous, and they've kind of become surrogate parents. I love cutting flowers for all of their events and for them to give to friends."

Seed-on-Hudson now grows enough flowers to supply holiday pop-up markets, local restaurant customers, and CSA (community-supported agriculture) subscriptions, sold in four-week increments from spring to fall. Katie also runs the seed exchange for the Hastings Public Library, volunteers on her local Hastings Pollinator Pathway Committee, teaches

Having access to a high tunnel at her satellite garden has exponentially increased Seed-on-Hudson's capacity to grow more flowers.

56

gardening at the Weinberg Nature Center in Scarsdale, and offers garden coaching services for local homeowners. It is truly a floral-centric lifestyle that keeps her closer to home and gives her more time with two now-teenage daughters.

Even though Katie hadn't planned on building wholesale channels, when florists in New York City and Westchester County learned that she was growing dahlias and chrysanthemums—and that the high tunnel at her satellite farm yields blooms weeks later than Hudson Valley farms (due to early frost there), she quickly responded to their demand. "These florists would just show up with their buckets and ask, 'Can I take all of this? Just send me a bill!'" Katie was especially surprised at designers' response to flowering tobacco (*Nicotiana alata*), an annual that blooms from late summer into fall. "It is so

hardworking and it doesn't mind the cold, so it's easy to grow," she notes. "And all the designers love it because it's so fragrant and very popular in bridal bouquets." Flowering tobacco is too fragile to ship, so there is little competition from imports or even from other growers in the United States.

Katie has recently returned to her pottery wheel after many years, focusing on wheel-thrown and hand-built vessels designed to accompany fresh or dried flowers.

Katie says her approach to pottery is similar to nursing a plant from seed to flower, and back to seed. She loves the visceral process of shaping clay into a solid form that can be cherished and reused for years or simply broken down and recycled. "Broken pottery makes great drainage material for the bottom of newly potted plants," she points out.

Opposite and above: Katie's return to the pottery wheel after decades was motivated by her desire to create vessels to contain the flowers she grows. Together, the clay and blooms make a lovely pairing.

FLOWERING TOBACCO

Nicotiana alata, Nicotiana × sanderi, Nicotiana langsdorffii, cultivars and hybrids

18"–38"
Light Shade to Full Sun
    (prefers shade from hot afternoon sun)
Perennial

FAVORITE VARIETIES
Nicotiana alata 'Lime Green', 'Grandiflora',
    'Scentsation', 'Crimson Bedder';
Nicotiana glutinosa;
Nicotiana langsdorffii 'Bronze Queen', 'Lemon Tree';
Nicotiana mutabilis;
Nicotiana rustica;
Nicotiana × sanderi 'Avalon Lime-Purple';
Nicotiana × sanderi 'Perfume Deep Purple';
Nicotiana sylvestris

An old-fashioned charmer, flowering tobacco belongs in the summer garden, especially as a tall beauty near the back of the border. Lightly fragrant, this cut flower adds a romantic touch, with its graceful stems and star- or bell-shaped blooms in dusky shades of mauve and pale green.

The genus is named after Jean Nicot de Villemain, a sixteenth-century French diplomat and scholar who is credited with introducing tobacco (*N. tabacum*) to the French court, where it was valued for its medicinal properties. Flowering tobacco is ornamental and is not grown for medicinal purposes (all parts of this plant are toxic if ingested).

First cultivated for its scent, nicotiana is a favorite for nighttime (or moon) gardens, as many varieties open their flowers at night, releasing subtly fragrant notes of jasmine. Newer cultivars offer other must-have features, including a wider array of petal colors, stem lengths, and bloom sizes and shapes. The leaves are typically sticky, and the flowers are displayed on tubular necks, making it easy for hummingbirds to feed on their nectar.

Below: Katie's whimsical annual nicotiana flowers are popular with her floral design customers, who value them for the delicate sense of movement they add to arrangements and bouquets.

Above: Beyond raising cut flowers in her residential garden, Katie has expanded Seed-on-Hudson's production to a historic home and garden located along the Hudson River.

WHEN TO PLANT
Start the seeds indoors, 8 weeks before the last frost. Or plant outdoors, just after the last frost. Press seeds into the surface of moist soil or planting medium; do not cover, as they need light to germinate.

WHERE TO BUY
Nicotiana plants can often be found at nurseries and specialty garden centers in the annual or cottage garden section. Many reputable seed providers offer a range of nicotiana seeds, including:
> *Baker Creek Seeds, rareseeds.com*
> *High Mowing Seeds, highmowingseeds.com*
> *Hudson Valley Seed Company,*
>   *hudsonvalleyseed.com*
> *Johnny's Seeds, johnnyseeds.com*
> *Select Seeds, selectseeds.com*
> *Strictly Medicinal Seeds,*
>   *strictlymedicinalseeds.com*
> *Uprising Seeds, uprisingorganics.com*

HOW TO WATER
Water the root zone regularly, especially during dry, hot spells.

WHEN TO HARVEST
Harvest when the first flower on a stem opens in the early morning or evening, when summer temperatures are coolest. Cut low on the plant for extra-long stems. Nicotiana responds well to continual harvesting and, although spent flowers do drop, deadheading will stimulate reblooming.

Xenia D'Ambrosi

SWEET EARTH CO.

Xenia and Adrian D'Ambrosi moved to the village of Pound Ridge, New York, in early 2000, leaving behind a Manhattan apartment for an 1800s farmhouse. They continued commuting to Wall Street for many years, but then Xenia fell ill and began her own version of horticultural therapy. "After my cancer diagnosis, I started to reconsider what I wanted to do and how I wanted to take care of myself and my family."

Xenia embraced eating locally and gardening. "I volunteered at some local farms, and I truly believe that having my hands in the soil healed me." She also studied at the New York Botanical Garden for a certificate in gardening with a focus on sustainable design and began to create edible landscapes for others in her community. She grew vegetables and herbs for her family and for private chefs, and eventually she formed Sweet Earth Co. A few years later, she added cutting garden design and transformed the kids' playfield into a farmstead, a thriving teaching farm filled with an acre of cutting flowers, which she grows for commercial use.

These changes may appear to be a 180-degree pivot for a born and bred Manhattanite, but Xenia can't help but think that her Puerto Rican grandparents would approve of her picking up the shovel and trowel. Her mother's family once farmed coffee and grew bananas and other fruit, and she's proud of the history of "land stewardship and farming that's ingrained in my DNA," Xenia confides.

Putting to use her MBA and marketing background, Xenia has since identified three themes that form the mission of Sweet Earth Co.: *We Grow. We Design. We Teach.* "For everything I do, I want to ensure that I'm connecting people with flowers and nature and communicating beauty and sustainability," she says.

The annuals, perennials, bulbs, and herbs that Xenia grows at Sweet Earth Co. are enough to supply their seasonal CSA (community-supported agriculture) subscriptions, fulfill custom wedding and event designs, and support the needs of her educational workshops. The number of CSA subscriptions, also called flower shares, continues to increase every season as local fans sign up for six-week spring shares (peonies, irises, tulips, alliums); eight-week summer shares (sunflowers, zinnias, strawflowers, cosmos, scabiosa); or nine-week late summer dahlia shares. A surprising number of flower fans order their bouquets for the season's entire twenty-three weeks.

Opposite: Xenia D'Ambrosi is a flower and herb grower, designer, and educator whose
Sweet Earth Co. is based on ecological and environmental values.

SWEETEARTHCO.COM | @SWEETEARTHCO

"Since I also offer an herb harvest, many folks add herbs to their orders, which I cut for them when they're here," Xenia says. There are more than twenty types of herbs growing on the farm, and customers can learn about the culinary and medicinal benefits of specific varieties before Xenia sends them home with their selections.

The flower shares introduce her customers to Xenia's other floral design and gardening services—from custom florals for private homes to container gardens and landscape consultations. It's all connected, she says. "When I'm installing landscapes, my customers want to know more about our flowers; when I sell flowers, people want to know how to grow them."

The loft above her barn is a welcoming studio space for consultations with wedding clients and for small-group workshops. The yearly calendar includes a Mother's Day bouquet class, dahlia season's "wine and design" party, and other holiday-themed events. These opportunities lure enthusiasts and put a face on the farm—something that Xenia believes helps change people's attitudes about sustainability in their own backyard. "They come with an open mind and an open heart—and get to make something beautiful with flowers or plants." She also teaches a Cultivating Sustainable Floristry workshop for professionals and hosts on-farm events for garden clubs, such as the Sustainable Herb and Tea Tour organized for a group of twenty-five. "They walked the gardens and flower fields and I discussed general land stewardship and sustainable gardening, the idea of mixing flowers and herbs in the garden, using herbs as cut foliage, and also using herbs for pest management. We visited my barn, where I have the herb-drying room, and I showed the attendees how we process the herbs and how to blend their own tea mixes."

She and Adrian met in business school and once had conventional financial careers; now, their respective MBA degrees are helping each partner pursue creative endeavors.

"Everybody wants to do something they are passionate about," Xenia says. "I am so blessed to be able to do just that. The name Sweet Earth came to me in a dream. The sweet earth here has improved my quality of life. I'm proud that we get to show our children that you don't have to go with the norm. You can do what you believe in, even if it's not the corporate world."

Previous spread: Jars filled with Sweet Earth Co.'s custom-blended herbal teas. Feverfew (*Tanacetum parthenium*). *Opposite*: The ritual of walking through the rows, beds, and borders to inspect her crops helps to ground Xenia in the healing gifts of nature. Here, a grassy pathway with two favorite perennials—purple coneflower (*Echinacea purpurea*) on the left and goldenrod (*Solidago* species) on the right.

HERBS

XENIA'S FAVORITE HERBS
(noted as A = annual or P = perennial)

Ornamental basil (*Ocimum basilicum*), (A):
bouquets and pollinators

Bouquet dill (*Anethum graveolens*), (A):
bouquets and pollinators

Feverfew (*Tanacetum parthenium*), (P):
bouquets, pollinators, and teas

Lavender (*Lavandula* spp.), (P):
bouquets, pollinators, and teas

Lemon verbena (*Aloysia citodora*), (P):
bouquets and teas

Mint (*Mentha* spp.), (P): bouquets, pollinators, and teas

Mountain mint (*Pycnanthemum muticum*), (P):
bouquets and pollinators

Oregano (*Origanum vulgare*), (P): bouquets,
pollinators, and teas

Sage (*Salvia officinalis*), (P): bouquets,
pollinators, and teas

Yarrow (*Achillea millefolium*), (P): bouquets,
pollinators, and teas

Below: A charming herbal bouquet is useful and aromatic.

Xenia considers herbs indispensable to Sweet Earth Co.'s flourishing floral business. "They are multi-faceted plants that can be used fresh in bouquets, but also dried for tea blends or for medicinal purposes. They are also an important element in our pest-management program."

The botanical definition of an herb is: an herbaceous plant that lacks a woody stem and dies to the ground each winter. Plants and plant parts used for culinary or fragrance purposes are also considered herbs. These are plants that satisfy all of the senses, valued for their usefulness in the cutting garden.

Many herbs, such as lavender, mint, oregano, sage, and yarrow, are perennials and return each season. Some tender herbs, such as all of the basils, are planted each year and are treated as annuals.

At Sweet Earth Co., Xenia integrates her herb plants throughout borders and beds, adding a verdant presence and many aromatic attributes to the landscape.

Above: Bouquet dill (*Anethum graveolens*).

WHEN TO PLANT

Herbs prefer organic, well-drained soil. Prior to planting, the area should be amended with compost. Herbs tolerate dry or hot conditions, as many species originate from Mediterranean regions. Annual herbs are started from seed and planted out after the last frost. Perennial herbs may be planted in spring. They are best planted as starts or propagated by taking cuttings or dividing existing plants.

WHEN TO HARVEST

Herbs are cut-and-come-again; when frequently harvested, plants will produce healthy regrowth. For use in bouquets, harvest the stems once they have flowered. Cut early in the morning or in the cool evenings and plunge the cut stems into water as soon as you can. To prevent wilting, condition herb stems in fresh water for 12–24 hours.

HERBS AS PEST MANAGEMENT

Many herbs are also valued in the cutting garden for their assistance in warding off pests while encouraging beneficial insects. Basil deters aphids, spider mites, and thrips. Allium, dill, and coriander repel aphids and encourage beneficial insects. Marigold is effective at repelling aphids and whitefly. Parsley attracts predatory wasps that feed on aphids. Interplanting these herbs among highly valued cut flowers, such as roses and dahlias, is part of a successful and ecofriendly pest-management strategy.

the FLOWER
FARMERS

South / Southeast

Mandy & Steve O'Shea

3 PORCH FARM

Based in Comer, Georgia, about ninety miles east of Atlanta, Steve and Mandy O'Shea grow premium cut flowers that they ship overnight to buyers across the country and sell to locals who pick up orders in person. The couple has poured fifteen years into building 3 Porch Farm as a mission-driven floral enterprise based on their values of "Principles before profits." Steve explains, "We want this farm to be an extension of our ideals and our ethics, and we're trying to do something good in this world. Not something big, but in a small way, a business we can feel good about with our principles intact."

3 Porch Farm is a true partnership between Mandy, a Georgia native whose horticulture degree led her to food farming, and Steve, a California native whose background includes alternative energy and construction. They met after Steve had dropped out of a master's program, sold everything he owned, and (with a few friends), converted a school bus to run on vegetable oil. "We wanted to drive cross-country, kind of on a lark," he recalls. "We started doing all sorts of presentations and getting invited to talk about biofuel at universities, festivals, and even make TV appearances." A friend introduced them to Mandy when they

had a presentation in the Athens, Georgia, area, and she showed them around the place she farmed. "We hit it off and I stayed for a week," he adds.

Mandy was the first farmer he'd ever met in his peer group, and Steve was inspired to pursue farming. He accepted an internship on a fifty-acre organic farm in California, where he supported the four hundred–member CSA (community-supported agriculture) and became the vegetable oil mechanic for tractors and delivery vehicles. Mandy later came to California to work on a horse-powered vegetable farm and then managed vegetable and flower growing for a large California olive oil producer. The two friends became a couple. "We decided we were in love, we were probably going to get married, and we wanted to start a farm together," Steve says.

Their farm search began in Northern California and quickly expanded beyond, to more affordable places. "Three or four years into our search, Steve mentioned that of all the places we had considered, he really loved Athens," Mandy says. "Suddenly, that made total sense, and I knew that community would be right for us." She habitually checked real estate listings in the area, and one day, a nine-acre property in Comer, including a

Opposite: Mandy and Steve O'Shea, partners in life and business at 3 Porch Farm in Comer, Georgia.

farmhouse with three porches, popped up. "This place had been posted only a half an hour earlier," she says, marveling at their serendipity after a long hunt.

Adds Steve: "We made an offer, sight unseen, and flew out three days later. It was so far above and beyond anything we wanted. It had literally everything on our list, including the claw-foot tub."

From the prior owners—a professor and a botanical garden professional—Steve and Mandy inherited an established ornamental landscape and some tools and equipment. Today, they farm on about five and one-half acres of the land, including three-plus acres dedicated to hellebores, peonies, garden roses, lavender, daffodils, and dahlias, and several high tunnels and hoop houses for the spring anemones, ranunculus, poppies, and fall chrysanthemums.

Although 3 Porch Farm had regularly sold at three farmers' markets around Athens and Atlanta and delivered wholesale orders to area florists, the sudden onset of the COVID-19 pandemic in March 2020 changed their entire business model. At the time, the high tunnels were exploding with spring flower crops, and farmers' markets had closed overnight, so Mandy and Steve quickly adapted. They used their newsletter mailing list and social media accounts to promote and ship flower-filled boxes across the country, gaining a following from flower lovers and florists hungry for fresh, seasonal blooms, especially during a time when supply chains were disrupted. 3 Porch Farm has since added hard-to-find hellebore seedlings, rooted chrysanthemum cuttings, and dahlia tubers to its shipping program. Local customers are still invited to shop at their Farm Store, which is frequently stocked with flowers, plants, and gift items, mainly by women artists, including pottery made by Mandy's mother, Linda Rovolis, and woodwork from her father, Tony Rovolis.

Mandy and Steve understand shipping flowers has an impact on the planet, and they address this concern by purchasing carbon offsets for every shipment. They process and chill flowers in solar-powered structures (the farm has 150 solar panels to supply all the energy it uses and feeds excess power back into the grid), and of course, they still use vegetable oil to fuel vehicles and farm equipment. Flower boxes are printed with soy-based ink so their customers can compost the cardboard.

Clockwise from top left: A dahlia garland embellishes the fence post to mark the path into the flower fields. Mandy, her mother, and a friend made floral garlands, boutonnieres, bracelets, and flower crowns for guests of their dahlia dinner. Years ago, Steve converted a used school bus to run on vegetable oil and drove it across the United States as a demonstration of an alternative fuel. Today, the iconic vehicle is a permanent fixture. When Steve and Mandy acquired the farm, they fell in love with an elderly dogtrot-style barn on the property. Steve reframed the mostly rotten structure bit by bit and added a workshop, packing facility, and a floral studio. In the foreground, the dancing *Lunaria* flowers (also called honesty or money plant).

At their annual retreat, Steve and Mandy often revisit the shared goals that formed the basis of their marriage and their farming business. "Every year, we identify the things that excite us and those we don't want to do anymore," Steve explains. "We aspire to be as close as we can to perfection with every single flower bunch we grow and ship. Shipping our beautiful flower offerings to retail customers (instead of investing so much time into special orders, events, or wholesale) means we're focused on growing the flowers and running the farm—and that feels good."

Those planning meetings take place in the vintage school bus that originally arrived at Mandy's place with Steve behind the wheel. "About six years ago, we flew back to California to pick up the bus and drive back to Comer," Mandy says. "Now it's on the farm to provide guest housing. But it's also where we go to get out of the house and away from daily demands. The bus reminds us of our free spirits, back when we first wanted to have a farm and live off the land. I love sitting inside with some tea, bundled up in blankets, with our pens and notepads, as we talk about what we want from life."

At left: Guests gather around farm tables stretching through the dahlia fields. The late-summer sunset event was a celebration of the season and helped raise funds for a special cause. *Following spread, clockwise from top left*: The shop brings customers to the farm, saving on delivery time and further connecting people to life on the farm. Claw-foot tubs from a local thrift store. Before Steve and Mandy had employees, the couple was fond of a cold-water plunge to stave off heatstroke during the hot and humid Georgia summers. Now, when they have the farm to themselves on weekends, the tubs are ideal for cooling off with a cocktail. The resident flock of guinea fowl provides chemical-free pest control. Endemic to Africa, the flock is also the main predator of ticks, preventing tick infestations and Lyme disease. They are low-maintenance, too, eating weed seeds and roosting in the trees. A simple hand-painted directional sign reads "3PF."

POPPY

Oreomecon nudicaulis
(common names, Iceland, Arctic, and Italian
[Colibri] poppy)

7"–16"
Full Sun
Moderate to regular water
Tender perennial grown as an annual

FAVORITE VARIETIES
Papaver nudicaule 'Champagne Bubbles Pink',
    'Champagne Bubbles Scarlet', and 'Hummingbird'

Below: Poppy harvest time takes place in spring, when the bright flowers lift spirits and promise a prolific season to come. Whether in bud form or full bloom, the flowers are irresistible.

Spring's most cheerful flowers come in a vivid spectrum of pink, orange, yellow, red, and creamy white, making the poppy one of 3 Porch Farm's most popular bloomers. Italian poppies and their associated Colibri seed line are cultivars bred and selected in Italy from the Iceland poppy, and are thus a subset of them. Recently reclassified from Papaver, the genus name *Oreomecon* is composed of two Greek roots, *oreo* = "mountain," and *mecon* = "poppy." Iceland poppy's native range is south and east-central Siberia to Alaska. These prolific perennials prefer cooler climates and are grown as early spring annuals in the South.

Mandy and Steve grow poppies under cover in the high tunnels. Plants are started from seeds or purchased as plugs, transplanted into 8-inch-high raised planting beds that stretch the length of the structure. Each bed accommodates six parallel rows of poppy plants, with drip tape irrigation. "This is such a great crop," Steve says. "We grow about 10,000 plants, which keep producing long after the first stem is cut. They grow longer than any other spring crop we have."

These poppy varieties produce blue-green basal foliage, formed as a 6-inch rosette. From this arises a thin, 7- to 16-inch-tall, hairy stalk, bearing cup-shaped flowers measuring up to 3 inches across when fully opened (5 inches for Italian poppy blooms). Florists value this flower for its unique form, which begins in

Above: Just-harvested poppies, with petal colors that favor the warm side of the spectrum, from creams and golds to pinks, corals, and oranges.

a bud resembling an oval egg encased in a shell and eventually cracks open to reveal the interior petal color. The shell can be coaxed off by hand to help the creped petals unfurl and reveal the button-like poppy seed pod at its center.

The bright flowers are a hit with local and mail-order buyers each spring, and many sign up for 3 Porch Farm's poppy subscription to receive thirty-five-stem bunches weekly throughout April. The farm recently introduced a pastel mix of the Iceland poppy, satisfying florist demand for softer palettes. The farm ships their flowers in the tight bud stage, with instructions that the flowers will quickly open once arranged in a vase and exposed to a home's warm environment. "People love watching poppies open—they're as enamored with that process as we are," Mandy says.

WHEN TO PLANT

In cold winter areas, sow seeds in earliest spring for summer blooms. Fall planting is recommended for early spring bloom. Prefers cool nights.

WHERE TO BUY

Flower farmers purchase plugs (small rooted starts) from distributors. Poppy seeds are often sold as mixes rather than a single variety.
Plugs:
  Farmer Bailey (Gro 'n Sell), farmerbailey.com
Seeds:
  Johnny's Selected Seeds, johnnyseeds.com
  Select Seeds, selectseeds.com
  Uprising Seeds, uprisingorganics.com

HOW TO WATER

Water regularly until plants are established and during dry spells.

WHEN TO HARVEST

Pick flowers close to the base of the stem when the bud is at the stage you prefer. 3 Porch Farm advises customers to ignore the lore about searing the poppy's cut stem. The Iceland and Italian poppy varieties do not need searing, Mandy notes. "After years of testing, we have found that a simple trim is best for making poppies last 5 to 7 days."

Sarah Jo Eversole

EVERBLOOM FIELDS

Just south of downtown Dallas, Sarah Jo Eversole's half-acre urban flower farm pumps out delicious blooms for a cohort of florists who value seasonal and local design ingredients. She is the primary farmer, supported by her husband, Matthew Eversole, who provides maintenance help. They live in an 1878 farmhouse with two young children, a son (age nine) and daughter (age seven), who are often found playing among the flowers while Sarah Jo tends to her crops. She named her farm Everbloom Fields as an extension of the family's surname, combined with a dose of "forever" optimism.

The scene sounds idyllic, but Sarah Jo will be the first one to say that flower farming in Texas is for one who is determined—and intrepid. "We have three long summer months where the temperature can exceed one hundred degrees every single day. It's really difficult to grow plants in that kind of environment. There's definitely a way to do it, but it can be intimidating at first."

Challenges ranging from winter ice storms and flooding to high summer temperatures reveal why there are only a handful of people who grow specialty cut flowers here, despite increasing demand from florists. "We are in a reverse situation to what you'd find in many other markets," Sarah Jo explains.

"The florists know about my flowers. They're actually pushing the movement forward, saying, 'Someone please grow more flowers locally.' Florists are competing with each other because there are so few flower farmers."

A native Texan, Sarah Jo loves the dirt, the sunshine, and science. "I grew up in a neighborhood that's a little bit like the one I live in now. There are a lot of struggles here, and people don't often have the resources or even the time to maintain a nice lawn. When I was a child, our yard was mostly dirt and a few pine trees. But there were also these beautiful azalea bushes that someone had planted years earlier. That bright pop of color against a dreary landscape was a promise—a promise that there was more beauty out there in the world. I just had to hold on; I had to get to it."

Sarah Jo studied science and statistics in college, which led to a career in data analysis. "I loved data and I loved flowers," Sarah Jo confides. After her second child was born with health issues, she left her technology profession behind. "I was home, sitting here with my little baby, and suddenly I had a big window of time. I didn't have a job and I was looking out on this piece of land, thinking about what I could do with it."

Opposite: Texas flower farmer Sarah Jo Eversole grows cut flowers for select florists who are eager to get their hands on locally grown blooms. She farms in an urban setting, taking full advantage of a "bonus backyard" where a field and high tunnel are filled with annuals, perennials, and bulbs.

EVERBLOOMFIELDS.COM | @EVERBLOOMFIELDS

On her shelf, along with nostalgic gardening titles by Tasha Tudor, was a book by Lynn Byczynski, a used copy of which Sarah Jo had purchased for seventy-five cents. "I pulled out Lynn's book and started reading about growing cut flowers. I told myself, 'I can totally do this.'" She joined the Association of Specialty Cut Flower Growers, an industry group, and dove into its website's archive of research. "It was like a unicorn moment because there it was—data, data, data. That was when my love of flowers and my love of data merged and blew my world open." From an entrepreneurial standpoint, Sarah Jo explains that the entry cost to become a flower farmer is relatively low. "With other businesses, you have all this expensive inventory to get started, but that's not the case with flower farming or even floristry. I just needed to buy seeds and find sales outlets."

Sarah and Matthew's residential garden had a "second back-yard," an adjoining lot, unused and large enough to plant rows of annuals and, eventually, to add a 1,700-square-foot high tunnel. "By my second year of flower farming, I intuitively knew that the plants needed protection because our weather is dicey. My husband and I built the high tunnel with the help of a couple friends. It paid for itself that season with gorgeous ranunculus, a crop that would otherwise rot because of our clay soil and wet winters." She now manages an entire rotation of bulbs and annuals inside the tunnel. Its sides are usually rolled up to allow for good air circulation, and drip irrigation provides a consistent source of water regardless of the weather outside.

Sarah Jo initially sold her flowers at the St. Michael's Farmers Market in Dallas but left because the timing of it was off. "The market started in late April and ran mostly through the summer, which is the hardest time to grow crops here."

That realization helped Sarah Jo shift her specialization to flowers that bloom between March and May. It's also the season when most Texas weddings take place and when local florists ask for Sarah Jo's blooms. Her early-season crops include ranunculus, butterfly ranunculus, peonies, snapdragons, stock, poppies, delphinium, foxglove, larkspur, lisianthus, and favorite delicate annuals such as feverfew and forget-me-nots.

Sarah Jo has partnered with her close friend Annamarie Jamison, who runs nearby Abundant Flower Farm, to market her harvest to local florists. "Annamarie has decades of experience in the floristry world. I mentored her in growing methods when she started her farm and she set up the florist delivery system." As a partner farm, Everbloom Fields' flowers are added to Abundant Flower Farm's availability list, sent weekly to florists. "I pay a percentage of my sales as a processing fee, which allows me to focus on farming high-quality flowers while she [Annamarie] handles the logistics," Sarah Jo explains.

"The florists know which grower everything comes from. In fact, they post photos of their designs to Instagram and tag each of us who provides their flowers. Even within the floristry world, there's a sense of collaboration. Our florists know that the choice they make—choosing where their flowers come from—impacts vase life, freshness, and the uniqueness that they can offer their clients. The relationship we have with them is really special."

Opposite: Sarah Jo loves to grow her annuals from seeds, because the practice gives her access to a wide selection of varieties. To sow snapdragon seeds, she uses trays, nurturing them indoors until they are ready for transplanting outside.

Above: A mix of 'Potomac' snapdragons, including 'Appleblossom', 'Pink', and 'Lavender'.
Opposite: Flower farming allows Sarah Jo to be home with her family, including her two young children. Her son is now old enough to lend a hand with many chores.

SNAPDRAGON
Antirrhinum majus

18"–30"
Full Sun
Prefers fertile, sharply-drained soil
 and cool temperatures
Perennial subshrub usually grown as an annual

FAVORITE VARIETIES
To beat the Texas heat, Sarah Jo prefers early
 blooming snapdragon varieties like 'Chantilly'
 and 'Costa'. 'Potomac' is also a well-rounded
 cut flower variety that performs well in heat.

Below: *Antirrhinum majus* 'Chantilly Light Salmon'

A storybook annual, snapdragons are cherished by gardeners and flower farmers alike. When grown as a cut flower crop (versus a bedding or border plant), the snapdragon fulfills the florist's need for "line" flowers, ones blooming as linear spikes with a profusion of tubular or butterfly-shaped blooms. Individual flowers are also said to resemble a dragon's head, which is why children love to pinch their sides to "snap" the not-so-ferocious mouths.

The mouth-like form is also reflected in snapdragon's botanical and common names. The name *Antirrhinum majus* comes from the Greek *rhis* ("snout" or "nose"), plus the Latin word *majus* ("large"). Translated, it means "looks like a big snout."

The native range of *Antirrhinum majus* is limited to southcentral France and northeastern Spain. They are usually pink in the wild, but the cultivated varieties are available in most flower colors except for blue. Modern cultivars are available in three forms: traditional (single-petaled); azalea (double-petaled); and open-face (single-petaled in an open array). Once considered a rather generic cut flower, snapdragons grown for the local floral marketplace (and not shipped) have a beautiful, full form that can add volume and soft texture to floral arrangements. The flowers are both fragrant and edible.

WHEN TO PLANT

Snapdragon seeds are miniscule and are best started in seed trays indoors. Sarah Jo starts 99 percent of her cut flower seedlings in fall to jump-start them for the spring season. Whether you sow seeds in spring or fall, start them indoors 6 to 8 weeks before transplanting outdoors. A grow light or shop light will aid indoor growth. The seeds may also be direct-sown into the garden once nighttime temperatures reach 50°F. Light is required for germination, so do not cover the seeds.

WHERE TO BUY

To grow the types of snapdragon favored by flower farmers, source seeds from online sources or from specialty nurseries. Here are some of Sarah Jo's go-to seed sources:

Johnny's Selected Seeds, johnnyseeds.com
Territorial Seed Company, territorialseed.com
The Gardener's Workshop,
    thegardenersworkshop.com

HOW TO GROW

Snapdragons will grow in any soil that is moderately fertile and well-draining. They prefer full sun to light shade and cooler temperatures. While they can tolerate a light frost, plants need protection if temperatures fall below 32°F. They can be planted as close as 4″ apart if a staking method is used. Alternately, when plants are about 12″ tall, you can pinch, or cut off, the top third of the stem for more blooms per plant and a more manageable stem length.

Above: Sarah Jo holds a mix of 'Potomac' snapdragons, including 'Appleblossom', 'Pink', and 'Lavender'.

HOW TO WATER

Snapdragons prefer consistently moist soil. Water at the base of the plants to ensure you don't knock over tall blooms. Watering in early morning will help prevent disease or sunspotting.

WHEN TO HARVEST

Harvest when florets on the lower third of each stem are open. Harvest in early morning before the heat arrives, to prevent wilting. Expect a vase life of 6 to 8 days.

Eileen Tongson
FARMGAL FLOWERS

The botanical lifestyle that Eileen Tongson leads today began with a simple packet of zinnia seeds from her mother. "In retrospect, I was very fortunate, because I didn't think much about it when I threw those seeds into some of my vegetable beds," she says. "But they grew like crazy!" Her parents, both nurses as well as lifelong gardeners, had inspired Eileen early on about the health benefits of growing vegetables. The proliferation of cheery zinnias in a rainbow of colors forever shifted her attitude about flower gardening.

She was once a nurse herself and taught undergraduate nursing students at the University of Florida. These days, as a farmer-florist and certified master gardener, she teaches gardening workshops and designs special-event florals for private clients, local restaurants and businesses, and national brands like Ford Motor Company, Chico's, Pama Liqueur, and JoJo's ShakeBAR.

Around the same time Eileen casually sprinkled zinnia seeds into her vegetable bed, friends invited her to join their new East End Market, a local food and restaurant hub where she raises flowers in the cutting garden and partners with Fleet Farming, an urban agriculture nonprofit, to maintain the market garden.

"They provided the space and the compost. I contributed the seeds, plants, and the womanpower," she says. The experience incubated FarmGal Flowers as a small agricultural business, as East End Market's owners and vendors encouraged her to sell blooms and teach flower gardening workshops. "When I'm working there, people ask for advice about their own gardens. I chat with families with children fascinated by the ladybugs and butterflies, and the bees we keep on the market roof."

The FarmGal Flowers home garden occupies a three-quarter-acre residential parcel in Winter Park, Florida, a suburb of Orlando where Eileen lives with her family. Her backyard produces a sunshiny palette of dahlias, zinnias, sunflowers, celosia, amaranth, delphinium, strawflowers, and herbs, and other heat-loving varieties fill her cutting garden and produce the blooms that supply most of her designs.

Raised beds face her recently completed Cottage, a 240-square-foot studio inside of which Eileen leads small-group workshops and teaches long-distance students online. Classes for larger groups occur at nearby venues—East End Market, Harry P. Leu Gardens, and the Edible Education Experience (a seed-to-table nonprofit)—and range from seed starting and

Opposite: Eileen Tongson, framed by a jasmine vine trained on a trellis.

cut flower growing to DIY floral design. There is a community of returning students eager for FarmGal's make-and-take workshops, which send them home with a succulent-planted design or their own seedlings, complete with care instructions. "Most of my students simply want to learn how to grow a flower garden like I have," Eileen says.

Florida's climate might feel inhospitable to cut flower growing, but the state is the largest producer of ferns and tropical foliage for the floral marketplace. Eileen's success at growing nearly year-round in Central Florida was once a curiosity; now it's part of her reputation. "Most of my students are home gardeners, not necessarily people who want to become farmer-florists. They're interested in learning how they can translate what I'm doing into their backyard spaces, to grow their own flowers to bring indoors or share with others."

Clockwise from top left: At East End Market, Eileen maintains the cut flower garden and frequently teaches customers about gardening and growing practices. The Cottage is surrounded by raised beds for growing cut flowers that occupy a corner of the three-quarter-acre property. With a modern-style shed roof and deep covered porch, not to mention a restroom and air conditioning inside, the charming structure represents Eileen's long-held dream of having her own studio, separate from the family home. A bee finds its way to feast on the pollen of a single dahlia growing in a bed near the Cottage. The presence of insects, birds, and other wildlife is a testament to the sustainable growing practices used here. The cutting garden is a tapestry of blooms, including a mix of butterfly ranunculus, foxgloves, and delphiniums.

Above and opposite: Inside the Cottage, which Eileen calls her "happy place," all sorts of creative activities take place, from private workshops and online courses to sorting seeds, drying flowers, writing, and reading.

CELOSIA
Celosia argentea and cultivars

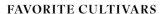

12"–48"
Full Sun
Drought and heat tolerant
   (low to moderate water needs)
Annual

FAVORITE CULTIVARS
Plume and crested celosia forms are cultivars
   of *Celosia argentea*, properly placed in groups
   as "Cristata Group," "Plumosa Group," "Spicata
   Group," and others.

Below: Eileen loves *Celosia argentea spicata* (Celway series) and *Celosia argentea* var. *cristata* (Plumosa Group). She says the soft cream, peach, and pink varieties are excellent design ingredients and blend well with most companion flowers.

Plenty of common names reflect the various forms of this easy-to-grow annual, among them cockscomb, crested cockscomb, Prince of Wales's feathers. Cultivars produce two flower forms—plume-like shapes and crested or fan shapes. Celosia is an amaranth relative. The name *celosia* comes from the Greek, *keleos*, meaning "burning," a nod to the genus's original flame-like bloom. This flower was a favorite of the Victorians, who ascribed boldness and courage to its meaning.

Eileen gained an appreciation for the flower after her first effort to grow 'Flamingo', a purple-magenta plume celosia. "As I discovered more color options, textures, and shapes, I couldn't imagine living without my celosias. I find their shapes so amazing. How does nature do that?"

Eileen collects seeds from all of her celosia plants, many of which self-sow in her cutting gardens. "I don't separate them when I put them [the seeds] in jars; the colors are all mixed up so I don't even know how many varieties I grow right now. I only buy new seed when there's a new variety that comes out." She counts both pastel shades (lemons and blush pinks) and brighter hues (orange, hot pink, magenta, and yellow) as equally useful in floral design. "Celosia is a great supporting flower for FarmGal's arrangements. In the fall, I tend to use the deeper colors, while in

Above: Spread across the worktable like floral confetti, plume-shaped and crested celosia flowers are ready to be added to wearable botanical pieces.

the spring, softer colors are popular. In addition to using celosia in bouquets and arrangements, I use the flower in our wearables—boutonnieres, corsages, and flower crowns. They don't wilt out of water and the color holds. It also dries well, so I use celosia for wreaths and other dried floral projects."

WHEN TO PLANT

In FarmGal Flowers' central Florida cutting garden, celosia is a year-round annual crop. Gardeners should direct-sow celosia when soil temperatures reach 70°F; otherwise, start seeds indoors for transplanting after last frost. Pinching is recommended to encourage branching. Low temperatures and less than 12 hours of light can cause premature flowering.

WHERE TO BUY

It's possible to find mixed-color packs of celosia at garden centers, but these are usually short-stemmed and are treated as bedding plants. Most growers start celosia from seed in order to access a wide variety of flowers. Seed sources vary widely. Here are some that Eileen uses:

Eden Brothers, edenbrothers.com
Floret, floretflowers.com
Johnny's Seeds, johnnyseeds.com

HOW TO WATER

Water regularly, and do not allow the soil to dry out.

WHEN TO HARVEST

Celosia is exceptional as a cut flower and can be used both fresh and dried. Fresh: Harvest when the flowers are fully developed and stems are firm at the base of the bloom. Dried: Harvest at the same stage of growth as you would for fresh flowers. Remove all the foliage and hang in a dark, well-ventilated location to dry. This helps the flower retain its color.

Holly Heider Chapple

HOPE FLOWER FARM & WINERY

Holly Chapple spent her childhood surrounded by plants, so it seems fitting that she is now the steward of Hope Flower Farm, a twenty-five-acre hub for all things floral. She describes herself as a farmer-florist. While the garden is her stage, its performers are her floral arrangements, lush and textured gatherings of the seasons throughout the year.

"I am a designer first, and I sustain my farm so that I have the stems I want for my designs," she explains. "I've always harvested from the garden. And now, I don't ever want to design without my farm as my source of inspiration."

After operating a full-service wedding and event design studio for many years, Holly and Evan Chapple purchased a historic dairy farm located just a few miles from their home. At Hope Flower Farm, all the threads of Holly's creative life in flowers are now woven together. The property produces acres of botanicals for her floral design studio and serves as a home base for teaching and mentoring, as well as a destination and hospitality venue for festivals and conferences. "It has become the heart of the whole company," she notes. Admittedly, it was a financial stretch to purchase Hope Flower Farm, and she credits a few "angels" for helping with the down payment. "We were so afraid of the risk, but Hope saved us," she says.

Three weeks after they closed on the purchase, Holly and Evan hosted a design workshop with international floral educator Gregor Lersch. Months later, they launched Flowerstock, an annual floral design festival, complete with glamping tents in the fields, where attendees were housed. "This farm is fundamentally at the core of everything we do now, every idea that we pursue," she points out. It is a long way from the myriad Washington, D.C., ballrooms that Holly and her team festooned and flowered year in and year out while building a reputation as a top wedding floral studio.

Holly's journey began at Heider's Nursery, the retail garden center owned by her parents. Like many children of entrepreneurs, she was expected to help out—whether that meant watering plants, selling produce from the back of a pickup truck, or pinching back buds on thousands of the nursery's famous potted chrysanthemums.

Later, as a young mother, floral design came naturally to Holly. Arranging centerpieces for local events or making bridal bouquets meant that she could be home with her toddlers. And

Opposite: Holly Heider Chapple considers the garden her most abundant design resource. In spring, this means clipping blooms and branches that flourish just steps away from her studio.

HOPEFLOWERFARM.COM | @HOPEFLOWERFARM

long before she relied on floral wholesalers to supply her recipes, Holly stepped outdoors to gather from the garden or from her father's garden center. "Our home property was loaded with lilacs, peonies, spirea, hydrangeas, and viburnum," she explains, as she lists the spring-flowering branches that now are part of her signature style. "I began to see flowers in a new light. It wasn't about watering and tending to them anymore. It was about making beautiful arrangements with them."

That same approach continues at Hope Flower Farm today, although on a larger scale. Holly and Evan renovated the many buildings there, including the original stone manor house and a cottage called the Tenant House. The farm residences often lodge guest instructors, and the Tenant House is offered as an Airbnb rental to help offset costs of farming. The couple also restored three stately barns, coaxing the original character from each to create gathering spaces for conferences, receptions, and workshops.

Nothing makes Holly more content than remaining at the farm. The property accommodates a wide array of events, including conferences for Chapel Designers, a community and forum for fellow wedding and event florists that she established more than a decade ago. The pastoral landscape and agricultural buildings are a magnet for new business opportunities, Holly adds. "We've been hired to produce branding and editorial photo shoots here, we have a retail shop in the carriage house, and we now have a winery with a tasting room," she explains. With support from the local tourism board, Hope Flower Farm is viewed as a regional travel destination. Guests are invited for flower festivals that highlight seasonal crops like daffodils, tulips, peonies, sunflowers, and dahlias.

Much of this productivity was initiated by Evan, who assumed the role of head farmer when the couple acquired Hope Flower Farm. Holly and Evan had a small cutting garden and landscaping plants at the family's residence located down the road, but Hope Flower Farm and its expansive fields magnified the need to make their land productive. Evan soon planted thousands of annuals, perennials, bulbs, and flowering shrubs, varieties that reflected Holly's distinct design aesthetic but also helped make weddings more profitable, as the farm supplied the studio's floral needs.

The Chapple family lost Evan to cancer in 2022, but his presence is still felt in every aspect of the farm. "The farm is our family's livelihood and Evan's legacy. The buildings and tools had lost their purpose, but Evan and I brought things to life. I think about myself as a little girl in her father's chrysanthemum field, the one who didn't want to grow plants, yet now it is what I love so much," Holly says.

Opposite, clockwise from top left: The character of elderly farm buildings is captured in a weathered red-painted barn with a vintage six-paned window. A veil of cottage garden annuals dances in the foreground. The all-terrain vehicle provides a quick way to dash from the studio to the fields and hedgerows at the farm's outer perimeter. Clipping just what is needed for a workshop, wedding, or design commission helps avoid overharvesting. A view across with dahlias in the foreground and summer annuals to the right.

At right: The E Shed, placed in the center of the first garden that Evan Chapple planted at Hope Flower Farm. The architectural gem is surrounded by Evan's plantings, including ninebark, abelia, blueberries, hydrangea, viburnum, phlox, peonies, dahlias, clematis, and passionflower vine.

Following spread, clockwise from top left: Tables are set for a festive gathering in the Bank Barn; botanical chandeliers hang from the rafters overhead. Hope's Manor House, built in 1850, has been restored to its original character, complete with antiques and artwork. The long trestle table in the dining room seats up to twelve guests for a private event. The coveted Manor House pantry (aka prop closet) is a sight to behold, organized with open shelving so that the designer can access pieces for special events, editorial photo shoots, and workshops. A seasonal spring arrangement reflects favorite flowering elements: spiraea, lilac, peony, bearded iris, and tulips.

FLOWERING BRANCHES

FAVORITE VARIETIES

Abelia, Flowering fruit trees (apple, cherry, peach),
    Forsythia, Mock orange, Quince,
    Spiraea, Viburnum, Weigela

Below: Vanhoutte spirea (*Spiraea × vanhouttei*) is a hybrid of *S. trilobata* and *S. cantoniensis.*

Flowering branches are a harbinger of spring, both in the garden and in floral designs. Whether used in centerpieces, bouquets, or in large-scale installations, blooming branches are indicative of the season—they say *spring*.

Before they bloom, bare spring branches produce tiny buds that will eventually burst into flower. There are several stages at which the branches can be cut and used in floral arrangements, Holly says. "Flowering branches express the season. If you see them at any other time of year, they look out of place. They indicate the beginning of spring, but I also love their shapes and forms—they really make a design so beautiful," she says.

Holly is known for creating large statement pieces for weddings and events and loves using flowering branches to elevate the scale of an urn or pedestal vase. "These extended, arching branches change the line, the shape, and the composition of my designs," she says.

Holly also favors the delicate tips of flowering branches for centerpieces and seasonal wedding bouquets, using them to add structure and texture in harmony with soft spring perennials. To this day, she is inspired by plants from the landscape as harbingers of each season of the year. "Our first garden was loaded in lilac, spirea, and viburnum—and all of a sudden, after years of working for my parents' nursery, I saw flowers in a new light," she explains.

Flowering branches that are cut when still in bud have a longer vase life than ones that are already in flower, she advises. "Harvest them early and you can watch them come into fruition. You can leave them at room temperature to get the level of [bloom] openness you want."

WHERE TO BUY

Most specialty nurseries and garden centers stock flowering trees and shrubs, sold as bare-root specimens, as balled and burlapped plants, or in large pots. Familiarize yourself with the options that are recommended for your growing zone.

HOW TO WATER

Water regularly until the plant is established. Do not let newly installed shrubs and trees dry out.

WHEN TO HARVEST

The best time to harvest is in early spring, when the plants are either in bud or when the branch has just begun to bloom. If temperatures are very cold, bring the branches indoors to force their blooms to open.

At left from top: Preparing lilac boughs for a centerpiece in the dining room. An open window in the Bank Barn frames a basket of spring flowers and offers a vantage point for admiring the distant Virginia landscape.

the FLOWER
FARMERS

Central

Maria Lourdes Casañares-Still

MASAGANA FLOWER FARM

The word *masagana* means "abundant" in Maria Lourdes Casañares-Still's native language of Tagalog, and her Manitoba flower farm in the heart of Canada's prairie landscape clearly manifests abundance. "I view the resources we already have from a place of abundance rather than scarcity," explains the self-described flower grower, natural dyer, and experience guide, who goes by her middle name, Lourdes.

Mostly self-taught through experimentation with plants known to have natural dye, Lourdes also studied online as she developed the "Tinta Experience"—named for the Spanish word that means dye, color, or paint—as a way to market her flowers. As a result, Lourdes has attracted the attention of agricultural and tourism agencies that want to incubate experiential tourism in the province.

Lourdes's journey began when she moved from the Philippines to the Canadian city of Winnipeg in her twenties and worked in sales at a wholesale outlet that supplied the floral marketplace with imports. After she met her husband, Kevin Still, the two began growing food and flowers on the five-acre property where they lived near La Broquerie, about one hour outside of the city.

"After one year of growing food together, we wanted to turn the lawn into something more productive," Lourdes recalls. "Now we have 4,800 square feet of lawn converted into garden beds." As she considered what to grow in a climate that typically averages 102 frost-free days, flowers increasingly appealed to Lourdes. She soon discovered the usefulness and beauty of dye plants. Fresh or dried, there are many botanicals that give her a year-round supply, including marigolds, dyer's chamomile, coreopsis, and scabiosa. She sells these easy-to-grow annuals to gardeners, fiber artists, and makers, but incorporates most of them into her popular dye-plant workshops through the Tinta Experience.

Students spend a half day at Masagana Flower Farm, learning from Lourdes how to turn their lawns into garden beds and which plants and flowers she recommends growing, and picking flowers for their textile projects. She teaches them how to dye a silk scarf with the flowers they have picked and follows it with a surface design project to create an indigo-dyed cotton shawl. "At the end of our creative time together, we gather around the table for a Filipino tradition that revolves around food and celebration," she explains. "Most people who come here would say that they're not creative, so I've created a safe space for them to

Opposite: At Masagana Flower Farm in Canada, Lourdes likes to say that natural dyeing
is her favorite way to immortalize Manitoba's short and sweet summer.

MASAGANAFLOWERFARM.COM | @MASAGANAFLOWERFARM

express their creativity, because we are all born creative; the problem is that we don't nurture it enough."

Because of her short growing season, Lourdes has explored ways to expand into year-round programing. "I taught eighty-one participants during my first season, and I realized that my flower farm could be economically viable if I had a heated, all-season building for Tinta Experience workshops." She applied for and received a grant from Travel Manitoba, which boosted her qualification for business loans from the Women's Enterprise Center of Manitoba, and from Futurpreneur, a non-profit organization that provides financing and mentorship to aspiring young business owners. The grant funding and loans, combined with a crowdfunding campaign, helped to finance construction of a 22′ × 22′ studio, completed in spring 2023, now the Tinta Experience headquarters.

Nervous about taking on a loan and managing a construction project, Lourdes drew on her mentors' support. "It got really scary, but by the time the walls were rising during construction, I had an incredible feeling that the possibilities would outweigh the uncertainty. I knew that once the studio was finished, I could do more programing." And that is indeed what has happened with the little studio that's nestled in the wooded area of Lourdes and Kevin's property, adjacent to aspen trees.

Today, the seasons guide the workshop's offerings. During winter, Lourdes's climate-controlled studio hosts up to six students for two-hour versions of the Tinta Experience, and other makers and artists are often invited to teach there. By spring, the topics turn to dye-plant growing for gardeners. "I teach my process of starting seeds and discuss which varieties they can grow. Then we dye a small piece [of fabric] so the students experience the colors that they will get when growing these flowers."

At the height of summer Lourdes offers a packed calendar of lengthier workshops. In addition to providing for seasonal you-pick customers, she also grows indigo plants for special indigo-dying workshops and harvests other botanicals, such as bark, roots, and seeds, called whole-dye ingredients because all parts are used to produce the dye bath. "There is so much interest from artists who have a need for this material," she says. "I've now dedicated more than half of my growing area for natural dye products."

As Lourdes has developed her methods of extracting dyes and pigments for surface design and dye baths, she has discovered her personal artistic style. She sells naturally dyed silk scarves, cotton bandanas, and indigo-dyed pieces through seasonal craft markets around Manitoba. The Winnipeg Art Gallery recently commissioned her to produce three hundred DIY (do-it-yourself) dye kits for one of their fundraisers.

"My whole Canadian life of fourteen years has been a journey. I've come from not knowing the prairies and thinking it was a little boring here to now learning what this ecosystem is all about and how important it is, through my own farming practices." Students are inspired to take home lessons from Masagana Flower Farm and continue growing and using dye plants, Lourdes says. "Most of them are gardeners, so they now have a new way of interacting with their plants—and I want to encourage more of that with more people, one garden at a time."

Opposite: Fresh flowers, petals, and other botanical bits create a whimsical pattern across the surface of a silk scarf. After this ecoprinting step, the fabric is folded and rolled, burrito style, and then steamed on a rack over boiling water. *Following spread*: A variation of ecoprinting creates a mirrored floral pattern: Flowers are placed in a colorful design, covering one half of a damp silk scarf; the second half is folded over the first half to cover the flowers. The folded piece is then rolled tightly around a wood dowel and the bundle is secured with twine or jute before steaming. The Tinta Experience invites guests to visit Masagana Flower Farm for dye-your-own wearable art workshops throughout the summer months. A clothesline displays botanically printed silk scarves and one indigo-dyed shawl made by Tinta Experience students. The covered space adjacent to the garden shed is used as an outdoor kitchen for simmering pots of dye and hanging textiles to dry.

MARIGOLD

Tagetes erecta

(common names, Aztec marigold, Mexican marigold)

24″–36″

Full Sun

Prefers moist, loamy soil but is tolerant of poor soil
   if consistently watered

Annual

FAVORITE VARIETY

Tagetes patula (French marigold)

Below: Lourdes says dyeing with indigo turns her hands blue. "That's my hand color most days in the summer," she jokes. "I am in awe that the color blue, often seen in blue jeans, comes from plants. I'm even more in awe that we can grow *Persicaria tinctoria* (Japanese indigo) in Mantioba." She holds a marigold, a primary Masagana Flower Farm crop and a favorite dye flower.

Interest in dye sources that are natural rather than chemical has elevated the demand for a wide array of plants. The common marigold checks all of the boxes for a mustard-to-saffron petal spectrum. Cut flower growers also choose lighter (cream, pale yellow, and light green) to darker (mahogany and russet) varieties.

All Tagetes are native to Mexico. Exported by colonizers, they became so popular in India that they are often claimed as "their" native flowers.

The genus name, *Tagetes*, refers to Tages, an Etruscan deity and grandson of Jupiter who was said to have sprung from the plowed earth, much like the prolific growth of a marigold seed. Most of these upright annuals or tender perennials have so many petals (rays) that the center (disc) is obscured, and they resemble small carnations. Single-petaled forms of marigold resemble a small daisy with an obvious center. The foliage is dark green and aromatic. Heirloom gardeners often pair their marigold flowers with tomato plants, believing that the bitter-smelling marigold foliage repels pests. This has not been proven scientifically, but it's a popular tradition.

Lourdes selects marigolds that have shorter days to maturity to get the most of Manitoba's limited growing season. She uses individual flower heads and unique petal color to create vivid colors and prints for silk and cotton. The flower heads can be simmered in pots of water to make dye baths. Lourdes varies the soaking time until she achieves the desired dye shade

Above: Students who participate in the Tinta Experience fill small baskets with blooms and petals for their silk scarf-dying project.

in the fabric. Fresh or dried flower heads of marigolds are also ideal for ecoprinting and bundle-dyeing, methods that transfer a flower "print" directly from the flower head or petal to the wet fabric, which is then folded or rolled and then steamed.

WHEN TO PLANT

Lourdes starts marigold seeds indoors, six to eight weeks prior to the last spring frost date in late May. She uses soil blocks for the seedlings, watering well until the first two sets of leaves emerge. The blocks are moved to an unheated greenhouse to harden off before they are transplanted outdoors in the garden. Marigolds can also be direct-sowed, or transplanted as nursery starts once soil temperatures warm.

WHERE TO BUY

Gardeners can find marigold bedding plants at garden centers, but to grow a wide range of specialty and heirloom varieties, it's best to start marigolds from seed and grow them as annuals. Seed sources vary widely. Here are some that Lourdes uses:
United States:
   Grand Prismatic Seed, grandprismaticseed.com
Canada:
   West Coast Seeds, westcoastseeds.com;
   William Dam Seeds, damseeds.com

HOW TO WATER

Water regularly. Marigolds do not require fertilizing once transplanted.

WHEN TO HARVEST

Gardeners deadhead spent flowers to stimulate the production of new blooms, but if you are growing marigolds as dye plants, you won't need to deadhead. Instead, clip the fully formed flowers to use fresh or cut the marigolds with longer stems to bunch them and hang them upside down to dry for later use.

Josh & Lindsey McCullough
RED TWIG FARMS

Josh and Lindsey McCullough own Red Twig Farms in central Ohio, where they grow cut flowers and woody shrubs and operate a nursery specializing in peony roots, potted peonies, tulip bulbs, and dahlia tubers. Ohio natives, Lindsey and Josh share a birthday (June 26) and were introduced by Josh's mother, Terri McCullough, who got to know Lindsey through the family's landscaping business and decided to play matchmaker. The couple married and later assumed full ownership of Red Twig Farms, combining their talents to grow the farm far beyond *Cornus sericea* (red twig dogwood), the original crop that inspired its name.

Having been raised in farming and horticulture, harvesting strawberries when he was young and planting gardens when he was in high school, Josh clearly has a green thumb. Lindsey claims she has a "black thumb," but brings her marketing and e-commerce expertise to the business. "Red Twig Farms was originally created as a division of the family's landscaping business, because we had a need for dogwood and willow branches for clients' holiday containers," Josh explains.

Inspired by the wedding market's peony craze, Red Twig Farms subsequently planted acres of peony plants, producing a second revenue crop beyond twigs. After they sold peonies at a Columbus, Ohio, area farmers' market for a few seasons, Lindsey saw an opportunity to change things up. "During the hot June weather at the farmers' market, our peonies were opening too quickly, so we were losing product," she explains. "I had a bet with my father-in-law that I could probably get shoppers to come to the farm—and I wanted to use social media to do it. We held a peony season 'opener' and 150 people showed up, demonstrating that there was a customer base willing to come to us." Because the peonies were kept chilled and fresh in coolers, buyers (and flowers) went home happy, she notes. By 2019, their fourth annual Peony Fest drew seven thousand people, who attended over Memorial Day weekend.

In 2020, forced to cancel Peony Fest due to shelter-in-place mandates, Lindsey and Josh faced fields planted with tens of thousands of tulips and peonies almost ready to bloom. They again turned to social media to help move their blooms, starting their Spread the Hope campaign, which invited customers to purchase and donate ten-dollar tulip bunches to support frontline healthcare workers, Meals on Wheels recipients, and even strangers in need of a gesture of hope. The campaign sold

Opposite: Lindsey and Josh McCullough, owners of Red Twig Farms at the beginning of peony season. Their high tunnel is filled with rows of potted peony plants whose buds are just weeks away from blooming.

REDTWIGFARMS.COM | @REDTWIGFARMS

and donated more than one thousand tulip bouquets in its first month. Customers continue to support the give-a-bouquet-to-a-stranger program, which enables Red Twig Farms to add a bonus bouquet in most shipments, with a note asking customers to spread the joy in their community, turning the once local campaign to a nationwide one.

The Peony Fest converted to a nationwide bouquet-by-mail program to market twenty-stem peony boxes. "We had four weeks to figure out shipping—learning how to best wrap our peonies in kraft paper to box them with ice packs," Lindsey says. "Since then, Josh has developed a special 'peony burrito' to protect the stems for shipping."

At the time, Red Twig Farms only had about ten thousand Instagram followers, but Lindsey felt social media was the best way to build a customer base outside of Ohio. Through posting images of voluptuous bunches of blooms, as well as "real" farm images of Josh planting and digging, they brought life on the farm to flower lovers' feeds. The account has grown six-fold during subsequent seasons, and Red Twig Farms' quarterly newsletter now reaches nearly fifty thousand subscribers.

Today, most of the tulip and peony bouquets are preordered by these Red Twig Farms fans, with only a fraction of their tens of thousands of peony stems going to local florists each season. On two occasions (in fall and spring), local shoppers are invited to visit the farm and purchase their own peony plants, giving them a chance to tour the high tunnels and peek into the farm operations.

Field-grown peonies stretch as far as the eye can see.

With about six acres in field production, four high tunnels, and a 30′ × 100′ shade structure, the farm marches through the season with the goal of supplying its customer base nine months of the year with branches, cut flowers, plants, tubers, bulbs, and holiday greenery.

The year begins and ends with branch harvest in a variety of colors and textures for holiday containers and decor (pussy willow, curly willow, winterberry, and dogwood), while nursery plants (bare-root and potted peonies), dahlia tubers, and tulip bulbs are snatched up by mail-order and local customers. In the fields, tens of thousands of tulips and peonies bloom in springtime, followed by an explosion of summer dahlias.

Because they live on-site in a cozy farmhouse, Josh and Lindsey and their three goldendoodle pups are never too far from the demands of the flowers. They schedule short day trips or long weekend breaks, leaving Red Twig Farms in the care of three full-time crew members and more than a dozen seasonal workers who show up for special projects, including the tulip and peony harvests, bulb shipping, and a favorite project: holiday wreath making.

"We've decided that remaining a 'niche' farm is what our customers want from us—and we're happy with that," Lindsey says. "Instead of trying to grow everything, we want to stay good at very specific things."

At left from top: Inspecting the peony crop for the coming harvest. Curved PVC pipe is placed along the plant rows as a support for cover cloth in the eventuality of a late frost. Josh McCullough works on the spring propagation, a familiar task for many peony farms. He digs up large peony roots, cleans off excess soil, checks for the presence of damage or disease, and then divides the clump into multiple bare roots for replanting or sale to gardeners. *Opposite*: A peek into the cooler, where mixed peony bouquets are ready for a Red Twig Farms peony festival.

PEONY
Paeonia lactiflora and cultivars

24″–33″
Full Sun
Prefers fertile, well-drained soil but can
 tolerate many types of soil
Perennial

FAVORITE VARIETIES
Paeonia lactiflora 'Angel Cheeks', 'Best Man', 'Coral Charm',
 'Coral Sunset', 'Fantastic', 'Karl Rosenfield', 'Mother's
 Choice', 'Red Charm', 'Sarah Bernhardt', 'Sweet Sixteen'

Below: 'Red Charm' peonies in full bloom.

There's nothing more alluring than a peony, a perennial favorite for May wedding bouquets and Mother's Day arrangements. During the four weeks when the peony blooms each spring, it entices the flower lover at all its stages—from the ball-shaped bud to the attractive, glossy green foliage, to the fluffy, 6- to 10-inch flowers.

There are two mythical stories attributed to the flower's naming. In one, Paeon, physician to the gods, extracted a milky liquid from the peony's root, curing Pluto. Another Greek myth is about the nymph named Paeonia, a beautiful maiden who captured the attention of Apollo and turned bright red and became shy upon being watched by Aphrodite. Admittedly, these are nostalgic plants that thrive for decades, inspiring a following among floral designers and clients alike. We can't get enough of them!

Paeonia lactiflora is a species of herbaceous perennial that is native from southeast Siberia to northern and eastern China and grows from thickened or tuberous roots. It grows well in a range of cold-winter climates, including Alaska and across the Northern Hemisphere. Gardeners and flower farmers in the South select heat-tolerant varieties for their regions.

Peony plants generally take up to three years to produce prolifically. If you wait until season three or four to begin harvesting, your plant will be healthier and a more vigorous bloomer. Plants should be staked or supported to keep blooms upright.

WHEN TO PLANT

Bare-root peonies are ideally planted in fall, while potted peonies (container grown) can be planted in the fall or spring. Situate the plant where it will receive at least 8 hours of full sun per day, in well-drained soil, in an area that receives good airflow. Peonies can be planted approximately 3′ apart. Prepare the soil by removing weeds and working in aged compost or leaf mold (chopped, composted leaves) throughout the top 6″ of the planting area.

Plant the peony with root tips pointing downward and the "eyes," or growing points, ½″ to 2″ deep. In colder climates, plant on the deeper end of this range; in warmer climates, plant more shallowly. Backfill the planting hole, taking care that the root crown is no deeper than 2″. Water generously, soaking the soil to eliminate air pockets around the roots.

Follow the same instructions for potted peonies, ensuring that the root crown is no deeper than 2″ below the soil's surface.

WHERE TO BUY

Most nurseries and garden centers offer potted peony plants. Bare-root peonies are often available through specialty mail-order nurseries. Take care to buy plants or roots from a reputable nursery source to avoid the spread of diseases.

Red Twig Farms, redtwigfarms.com

HOW TO WATER

Fall and winter rains typically provide enough irrigation for the bare-root plants.

Above: 'Bunker Hill' is a stunning, red-rose peony that has been in the floral trade for decades. A proven performer, it's a good choice for residential landscapes and cutting gardens.

In spring, water regularly during dry spells, especially before peonies bloom. Overwatering can cause crown rot or other disease issues.

WHEN TO HARVEST

Flower farmers harvest peony stems at the "marshmallow" stage (when a gently squeezed bud feels like a marshmallow). At Red Twig Farms, this is the preferred stage for shipping cut peonies. Once cut, the stems should be immediately placed in water. The buds will begin to open with the warmth of an indoor space. Gardeners can cut their peony stems when the buds are partially opened. Cut at the base of the stem for extra-long length.

Gretel & Steve Adams

SUNNY MEADOWS FLOWER FARM

Gretel and Steve Adams, together for more than twenty years, are far younger than the average US farmer. Yet these first-generation flower farmers, without an agricultural background, have spent nearly two decades building Sunny Meadows Flower Farm into an enterprise. The farm encompasses more than thirty acres, employs twenty-eight people, produces tens of thousands of floral stems each year, delivers bouquets to local Columbus customers, supplies florists and retailers across Ohio, and ships flowers far beyond the state through a national wholesale program.

It was a much smaller venture when, in 2006, Gretel inherited a small cottage surrounded by ten acres, located just outside the city limits of Columbus. For the couple, Sunny Meadows represented a dream of farming together and a tribute to their mutual love of nature. Early on, they grew equal amounts food and flowers to sell through a community-supported agriculture program, eventually learning about flower farming after Steve apprenticed with a market grower who raised sunflowers, zinnias, and cosmos to supplement his teacher's salary.

"We quickly realized how much money we could earn with our local flowers," Steve explains. "We found this niche that no one else was really doing in Columbus, and we went for it. What we earn per acre on cut flower production is dramatically different than what we were doing with vegetables alone." Gretel agrees: "Over time, we were just pulled more toward growing one hundred percent flowers."

With leased parcels in and around Columbus added to their original ten-acre farm, the floral operation has grown like a patchwork quilt. At the home farm, you now can find mostly woody and herbaceous perennials such as hydrangeas, viburnum, willows, yarrow, and sea oats tucked into the corners. There are also more than one dozen greenhouses that produce luxury crops like ranunculus, anemones, freesia, and lisianthus, plus a farm store open to the public. The leased farmland has been essential to meet demand from wholesale customers (grocery chains and florists), with vibrant rows of field-grown annuals (celosia, amaranth, sunflowers, and zinnias) and lots of dahlias.

The promise of a new permanent home for their crops was recently achieved with the purchase of thirty acres of land, complete with a house. The investment allowed them to relocate, a move that coincided with the birth of their first child, Levon Wyatt Adams.

Opposite: Gretel and Steve with Pinto, the farm dog, in front of a mural by the artist Miss Birdy (Mandi Caskey).

SUNNYMEADOWSFLOWERFARM.COM | @SUNNYMEADOWSFLOWERFARM | @FLOWERFARMER | @FLOWERFARMETTE

Intuition and risk-taking are part of Steve's DNA, Gretel says. "His brain really thinks in systems and he is very future-oriented. He drives the change here. He's the idea person. I'm the one who figures out how to fit those ideas into what else we have going on." They manage the farm together, with Steve handling the growing operations and field production, while Gretel oversees the barn crew, bouquet making, and sales.

They expanded outside the Columbus market by distributing Sunny Meadows' bouquets to a Cleveland-based grocery chain with twenty-three stores. "We looked for a chain that had a distribution center that we could deliver to," Steve says. Sending a truck filled with their flowers to Cleveland each week also gave Sunny Meadows a chance to connect with florists and flower shops there, building another channel for their flowers. Similarly, the farm has built a Cincinnati route to serve florists in that market.

Sunny Meadows sells flowers far outside of Ohio, direct-shipping to florists and farmer-florists around the United States. The program began with their early season ranunculus, which bloom at a time when demand is high and the availability of locally grown flowers is low, Gretel explains. "We gain new customers when it's ranunculus season. That's our biggest customer acquisition time, because ranunculus is so popular, it ships well, and it lasts a long time in the vase." Sunny Meadows kicks off the season with a rainbow of ranunculus varieties, including pastel and primary-colored ones and unique picotee forms with flecked margins.

Selling wholesale to florists around the United States is a "train we can't even really slow down," Steve observes. Customers include retail flower shops and wedding and event designers and, surprisingly, other flower farmers who need to supplement their own crop mix or extend their seasonal offerings. The wholesale shop has expanded to include other in-demand event flowers, like tulips, anemones, lisianthus, and dahlias, as well as collections of mixed blooms.

Gretel and Steve are no longer the beginners when they attend farming conferences, but they are the ones asked to teach and speak. "We've learned so much from our mentors," Steve says of the many growers the couple knows around the country. "We wouldn't be where we are today if people hadn't been so generous with their knowledge. Flower growers are a different breed altogether."

Opposite, clockwise from top left: The zinnia harvest underway. A truckload of flowers moves from the fields to the barn, where blooms are processed and bunched to fulfill legions of orders. The field crew gathers and bunches sunflowers, making sure to cut the stems as long as possible to meet customer expectations. The promise of blooms to come is captured in these tiny lisianthus plugs, lined up and ready to plant.

Above from top: Open to the public as a retail flower shop, the farm stand is stocked with fresh bouquets and single-variety bunches, dried flowers and wreaths, and gifts. Flowers are bunched and hung upside down from the rafters to dry at Sunny Meadows' barn, providing an important revenue source after the first frost. *Opposite*: The annual celosia crop. Celosia is a favorite design ingredient for Sunny Meadows' bouquet program.

RANUNCULUS

Ranunculus asiaticus
(common name, Persian buttercup)

12"–18"
Full to Part Sun
Prefers moist soil and cool temperatures
Herbaceous perennial grown as an annual

FAVORITE VARIETY
Ranunculus 'Elegance Bianco Striato'

Below: This favorite 'Amandine Purple Jean' ranunculus has a variation of petal colors resembling brush marks that range from light lavender blush to deep magenta.

According to a Persian legend, a handsome prince wearing garments of green and gold fell in love with a beautiful but haughty nymph. He sang to her and tried to woo her, but she rejected his advances. The prince eventually died of a broken heart, and a ranunculus grew from the spot where he fell. In an alternate version of this myth, other jealous nymphs tired of his serenade, so the object of his affection turned him into a ranunculus.

Like the mythical prince, Steve and Gretel are also mesmerized by this flower, but their love for ranunculus is perhaps more pragmatic. This multipetaled bloom is produced by a modified stem called a *corm*. The Ranunculaceae family encompasses some four hundred species of annuals, biennials, and perennials, many of which are cultivated hybrids, along with others that are found in the wild or considered weeds.

At Sunny Meadows, ranunculus corms are planted in December and January and harvested between March and April. Forty thousand ranunculus blooms represent a financial windfall, as the timing coincides with the end of winter's dormancy. The farm can barely meet florists' and flower lovers' demand for this dazzling bloom, valued for its beauty at a time of year when few other focal flowers are available from US farms. "We have amazing-looking ranunculus," Steve says.

When ranunculus burst forth in the greenhouses, locals pick up bunches from Sunny Meadows' farm stand as a rite of spring. Wholesale customers across the United States order bunches for overnight

Above: Masses of ranunculus in bright pastel colors and saturated ruby tones have mesmerized florists and flower lovers and are appreciated for the focal role they play in floral design and for their long-lasting vase life.

shipments to regions where these charmers are hard to find in quantity. To propagate ranunculus, Sunny Meadows' farm crew separates mature corm clumps into individual pieces, each with a center stem.

Hybrid ranunculus blooms are uniform in shape, defined by hundreds of paper-thin layers of cupped petals arranged around a central dark eye. The finely divided ferny basal leaves emerge at the base of hairy stems ranging from 12″ to 18″ tall.

"The blush, white, and salmon-colored ranunculus are big hits for Easter and Passover; and then, as we close in on Mother's Day, customers want the orange, hot pink, and yellow varieties," Gretel explains. "It's always fun for me to mix the different colors together in a huge bunch."

Sunny Meadows grows specialty offerings, including Italian-bred 'Cloni Success Hanoi" and 'Elegance Bianco Striato', which Gretel loves for its tiger-striped margins that look as if the white petals have been dipped into a pool of dark violet ink.

The Dutch-bred ranunculus Romance series, with very large double blooms and tall stems, satisfy demands from florists who are looking for a peony-like bloom for well before peony season. Dutch breeders are also responsible for the butterfly ranunculus, a

"cousin," with its ruffled, delicate-looking single layers of petals in pastel hues, favored for long-lasting vase life. Butterfly ranunculus is completely different in form and appearance from the pillowy standard variety. Gretel says, "I love how they float, monarch-like, above all the other flowers in my bouquets."

WHEN TO PLANT
In warmer climates, plant ranunculus corms in fall for early spring flowers; in cooler areas, plant them in spring for summer blooms. Soak corms for approximately 6 hours before planting, to hydrate them. Plant in areas where they will receive full sun.

WHERE TO BUY
Ranunculus corms can be ordered from a number of online sources or found at specialty nurseries and garden centers. Order in the fall.

> *Longfield Gardens, longfield-gardens.com*
> *Sunny Meadows Flower Farm,*
> *shop.sunnymeadowsflowerfarm.com*

HOW TO WATER
Requires average water. Do not allow to dry out.

WHEN TO HARVEST
For florists, Sunny Meadows picks ranunculus just as they start to unfurl, "in the fluffy marshmallow stage, similar to peonies," Gretel says, meaning that the buds feel like marshmallows when gently squeezed. For their retail customers, the farmers allow the flowers to open further but not fully.

Mimo Davis & Miranda Duschack
URBAN BUDS: CITY GROWN FLOWERS

Farmer-florists Miranda Duschack and Mimo Davis grow on one very busy acre known as Urban Buds: City Grown Flowers, in the Dutchtown neighborhood of St. Louis, Missouri. As cofounders, friends, and business partners, they have created a sensory oasis that provides more than eighty varieties of botanicals to customers in their community.

While Urban Buds is an equal partnership formed in 2012, its roots date to the mid-1990s when Mimo operated Wild Thang Farm in Ashland, Missouri. She was a social worker in New York City when she came to Missouri for a family wedding in 1989 and spotted the real estate classifieds in a local newspaper. "I was living in a studio apartment, paying $1,500 a month in rent in New York," she recalls. "I realized I could have a fifteen-acre farm in Missouri for the same amount of money. I was ready to retool myself and I recall saying, 'I want a different life.'" Her move led to studying agriculture, working for a native plant nursery, and starting Wild Thang, a four-acre flower farm that employed a small crew and supplied florists in Columbia and St. Louis. In the early 2000s, Mimo leased her farm and left for graduate school to obtain her master's in horticulture, which brought her to St. Louis, where she and Miranda met.

A Wisconsin native, Miranda had been working in food farming for New Roots Urban Farm in St. Louis and as a small farm specialist for Lincoln University of Missouri's Cooperative Extension (LUCE).

A phone call led the women to their future farmland in 2012. At the time, both were working as Cooperative Extension educators for Lincoln University of Missouri, an HBCU (historically black college and university). "Someone contacted Miranda to let her know that they were trying to sell this property with a glass greenhouse, so she suggested we go take a look at it," Mimo recalls. "All I could think of was, 'A greenhouse in the middle of the city? How's that possible?'"

The property was vacant and condemned, but, says Mimo, "I walked in and took one look, and said, 'Miranda, this is ours.'" Their purchase acquired four city lots, including the Lord & Burnham glass greenhouse, a glass propagation house, and an attached flower shop dating to 1904. Also included in the purchase was the dilapidated original 1870 farmhouse, which has since been demolished. Miranda and Mimo kept their full-time jobs with the university and invested their paychecks and sweat equity during weekends and evenings to restore the neglected flower farm and bootstrap it into Urban Buds.

Opposite: Miranda Duschack (left) and Mimo Davis (right), with their son, August Davis Duschack, during tulip harvest.

CITYGROWNFLOWERS.COM | @URBANBUDS

The farm sits on Osage Nation Tribal land. It was owned and farmed for food and flowers by the Held family for three generations, from 1904 to 1995. "Eighty years ago, they were true farmer-florists," Miranda notes. "The city grew up around this place." Today, Urban Buds is known for its restored greenhouse, an iconic glass, steel, and brick structure built in the 1950s and now filled with 2-foot-tall ranunculus, jewel-colored anemones, tulips, freesia, and other luxury blooms. "It's part of the reason we bought this property—a big part," Miranda says. "It feels so decadent to be growing under glass, and we love it."

Only seven miles from the city's most familiar landmark, the Gateway Arch, Urban Buds is a beloved neighborhood fixture. Subsequent structures have been added, including a high tunnel, which allows Urban Buds to produce St. Louis–grown cut flowers year round—a diverse lineup of bulb flowers, annuals, and perennials planted densely to maximize the 0.6 acre of actual growing space. "It's amazing how many flowers we can crank out of this little farm," Mimo says. "That's why urban farming is so fantastic for flower crops."

People living up and down Tennessee Avenue feel invested in this intrepid operation. "We're contributing to the community in a real way," Mimo acknowledges. "Urban Buds' presence here is encouraging people to participate in nature. People watch us and ask questions. They peer into the farm, and they're just blown away. The garbage man tells us how beautiful it is." In 2015, Urban Buds was named St. Louis's Neighborhood Business of the Year. "It feels so good that people support us," Miranda says. "They're starting to say words like 'urban farm,' understanding what that means. They want to come here and see it, which is one of the joys of farming in the city, because people have access to us."

The greater flower farming community looks to Urban Buds as a leader, and both Mimo and Miranda are in demand as speakers at regional and national specialty cut flowers and agriculture conferences. In 2023, the farm hosted a tour of hundreds of their peers as a featured stop during a meeting for the Association of Specialty Cut Flower Growers, a professional group in which Mimo serves as vice president. "That event was the pinnacle of my career," Mimo observes. The visibility has further propelled the women into education and consulting opportunities.

After experimenting with many sales channels for their flowers, today Urban Buds focuses on a few key outlets. The farm has had a long-standing presence at the Tower Grove Farmers Market in Tower Grove Park, where the women got started by selling mixed bouquets and single-variety bunches. "The farmers' market has provided a wonderful opportunity for us," Miranda says. "Our customers are so interesting. They range from people who buy three stems a week to [ones who buy] multiple arranged bouquets. We try to have something for everyone."

Opposite: Urban Buds occupies several residential parcels in St. Louis's Dutchtown neighborhood. Since Mimo and Miranda established their flower farm here in 2012, they have revived and revitalized the historic property.

When Urban Buds sells their flowers to florists, it's to studios and shops that value locally grown flowers. "Our flowers usually last twice as long as the florists expect," Mimo says. "Yes, they are priced higher than what a conventional wholesaler charges, but they are incredibly fresh." Mimo and Miranda care deeply about educating their floral community, as well as the wedding clients they serve. "We're growing the best quality flowers for their very best day. Their grandchildren are going to be looking at those photos someday—so the flowers need to be awesome," she says.

Miranda and Mimo's flower family is deeply interwoven. The women have a child together, and although they are no longer married, they continue to operate Urban Buds as a team. They have transitioned away from prior off-farm jobs, building the capacity of Urban Buds by extending the seasons and adding high-value floral crops. "We didn't want to get into massive debt but have grown Urban Buds with a pay-as-you-go approach," Miranda says.

They are well aware of their legacy, nurturing a decidedly modern, urban flower farm on the grounds of a nineteenth-century one. "Every day I wake up and think about Herman Held, the original founder of this farmland," Mimo says. "We honor him every day that we're working here. We're taking back the farm, one lot at a time, expanding into the neighborhood with more local flowers."

At left from top: Ornamental cabbage and kale in the greenhouse. Flowers and other botanicals for the floral market are grown both outdoors and under cover, taking advantage of the various microclimates at Urban Buds and producing crops on a year-round basis. *Opposite*: A crew member carries just-picked celosia, the extra-long stems of which tower above the rim of a harvest bucket.

ANEMONE

Anemone coronaria

(common names, poppy anemone and windflower)

10"–12"
Full Sun to Part Shade
Prefers well-drained, moist soil and cool temperatures
Corm grown as an annual or perennial

FAVORITE VARIETIES
Anemone coronaria 'Jerusalem Blue', 'Jerusalem
   Red', and 'Rarity';
Anemone coronaria 'Mistral Panda'

Below: Anemone coronaria 'Mistral Panda', a beloved anemone with a distinctive purple-black center.

Often grown as a companion to ranunculus, the anemone is an eye-catching spring focal flower, a tender perennial grown from a small corm.

Anemone coronaria is native from the Mediterranean basin east to Iran. The plant's name comes from the Greek word *anemos*, for "wind." According to Greek mythology, the flower sprang from Aphrodite's tears upon the death of Adonis, her lover. Red anemones (*Anemone coronaria*) are said to have blossomed from the ground where her tears fell. The flower is believed to symbolize good luck and protection against evil.

For flower farmers and gardeners, the good luck is that anemones are easy to grow and produce dazzling flowers. A buttercup relative, the anemone produces solitary, bowl-shaped blooms in a range of hues from white, pastel pink, and lavender, to supersaturated jewel colors of hot pink, crimson red, and purple-blue. The blossoms open wide to reveal intensely blue-black centers, especially notable in the 'Mistral Panda' form, which produces white petals around contrasting dark centers and is a favorite of brides. The lacy green foliage and tall, slender stems are a bonus.

In milder climates, it's possible to perennialize anemones to return in the spring, just like tulips or daffodils. Many farmers in colder regions grow their anemones under protective cover in a high tunnel or, like Urban Buds does, in greenhouse conditions.

At left: Of the many crops Mimo loves farming, the anemone is a cherished one, greeting the early spring season with its cheery blooms. "I've grown them for years," Mimo says. "Valentine's Day is when we really start to cut them. They make a beautiful bunch—in the jewel tones and the pastels."

WHERE TO BUY

Anemone corms can be ordered from a number of online sources or found at specialty nurseries and garden centers.

Dutch Grown, dutchgrown.com
Eden Brothers, edenbrothers.com
Longfield Gardens, longfield-gardens.com
Sunny Meadows Flower Farm,
  shop.sunnymeadowsflowerfarm.com

HOW TO WATER

Requires average water. Do not allow to dry out, but do not overwater.

WHEN TO HARVEST

Each plant is expected to produce three to four blooms. There is a little foliage "collar" that forms at the base of each anemone flower. When the stem between the flower and the foliage collar measures ½" to 1", it's time to harvest the anemone. Harvest early in the day. To get the longest stem possible, Mimo recommends a two-hand method of grasping the base of the stem with one hand while twisting and pulling with the other.

WHEN TO PLANT

In warmer climates, plant anemone corms in fall for early spring flowers; in cooler areas, plant them in spring for summer blooms. The corms will be rock-hard and require hydrating prior to planting, so soak corms for approximately 2–3 hours before planting. Mimo recommends soaking in a container that has some type of air circulation, such as a bubbler or a small stream of water. The soaked corms can be planted in trays and sprouted in a greenhouse; a heat mat is recommended. Or they can be planted directly into the garden or into containers in areas where they will receive full sun.

the FLOWER
FARMERS

West

Carly Jenkins & Jamie Rogers
KILLING FROST FARM

A food-growing hobby became a business for Jamie Rogers and Carly Jenkins when they named their Missoula-based backyard venture Killing Frost Farm during the first big frost of the 2014 winter season. The reference to a "killing frost," the extreme drop to freezing temperatures that can suddenly kill vegetation, also revealed a bit of grim optimism, Carly says. "It was a crazy time to start a farm, but I guess we embraced the challenges of our geography."

Like many who choose to grow flowers, Jamie and Carly began with vegetables and herbs. Both worked in other jobs (Jamie as a freelance writer and Carly as a hair stylist). Their edible garden soon expanded from their backyard to an adjacent city lot. In a state known for cattle and wheat, the embrace of cut flower farming could be considered an odd venture, but they planted sweet peas and cosmos along with the tomatoes and herbs, eventually converting Killing Frost Farm to a 100 percent floral operation.

They partnered with another Missoula grower, Katherine Sherba of Mighty Fine Farm, and formed a small wholesale flower hub in their garage. "I loved the community aspect of it," Carly says. "It made a lot of sense to help us succeed in an industry where we were trying to create a new market for our flowers. We wanted to increase the allure for local flowers and get florists excited." The flower hub allowed other beginning farmers to collectively offer customers more varieties and a consistent volume of flowers during the May through October growing season.

Although the Montana State Florist Association is quite active, there is no floral wholesaler located in the state, so the local flower shops were in the habit of ordering flowers from distributors and importers outside the region. Carly and Jamie wanted to target florists with their Montana-grown message and demonstrate that locally grown flowers were a beautiful alternative to products shipped in boxes.

Very quickly, Killing Frost outgrew the urban land parcels they had, and so Jamie and Carly relocated their farm. First they moved to a secluded parcel in Potomac, located about one hour west of Missoula, and then, in 2021, to what they now consider their permanent farm home in Helena. Their two-acre parcel of land in the fertile Prickly Pear Valley is surrounded by rolling hills and Mount Helena. They have doubled their growing operation and, unlike their prior location, it is close to city amenities, has access to well water, and is farther from the threat of fire.

Opposite: Carly Jenkins and Jamie Rogers have been flower farming in western Montana for more than a decade, shaping Killing Frost Farm into a boutique wholesale floral operation that grows annuals and perennials for professional florists and flower shops.

@KILLINGFROSTFARM | @FARM.TO.FLORIST.MONTANA

"We spent the better part of a decade white-knuckling things, trying to make our farm commercially viable," Jamie acknowledges. "And frankly, we did that at the expense of our well-being at times, and I think a lot of farmers probably have experienced something similar. The move to Helena was about creating a more holistic picture of our happiness and well-being."

The original Missoula flower hub has been reimagined as Farm to Florist Montana, a mobile floral wholesale program that supplies florists and shops across western Montana with an impressive botanical selection of cut flowers, from heat-loving annuals and perennials like sunflower, strawflower, stock, snapdragon, foxglove, scabiosa, zinnia, gomphrena, amaranth, marigold, cosmos, larkspur, Queen Anne's lace, sea holly, and delphinium; to bulb flowers like ranunculus, tulips, and dahlias; and specialty foliage like raspberry and eucalyptus.

Jamie and Carly credit much of the success of their current model on one developed by their mentors, Ralph Thurston and Jeriann Sabin, who for more than three decades operated Bindweed Farm in Blackfoot, Idaho. "They taught us that there's a certain size where wholesale really makes sense—and that's what we're striving for," Carly says, noting the efficiencies of marketing larger quantities of flowers to a small but consistent cadre of florists.

During the winter, Montana florists return to more conventional flower sourcing, ordering flowers from out-of-state suppliers. "Thanks to the long-term relationships we have built, our florists are willing to pivot back to us and away from their typical buying model during our five- or six-month-long season," Carly adds. "They get really excited about buying from local farms and being so open to what we grow. They know the quality of flowers that have not been shipped."

Killing Frost Farm put down permanent roots on a two-acre field in Helena, Montana. They divided the property into five blocks, including this one with ten planting rows. Each bed measures 3′ × 200′, yielding an incredible amount of blooms.

Opposite: Home sweet yurt. Carly and Jamie initially moved into a yurt at Killing Frost Farm. A more permanent residence may happen in the future. *Above from top*: The quintessential summer annual, sunflowers have proven their worth, especially with grocery buyers. The annual thrives in sixteen hours of sunlight each day, and Jamie and Carly direct-sow up to eight successions of sunflowers during the season. A storage shelf does double duty as a flower drying rack and a place for a favorite hat.

DELPHINIUM

Delphinium species and hybrids

36"–48"
Full Sun to Light Shade
Prefers rich, well-drained soil
Perennial

FAVORITE VARIETIES

Delphinium elatum Guardian series, which is densely flowered, and *Delphinium × belladonna* series, which has an airy form with open-faced blooms. Within each series there is a range of petal colors. Killing Frost Farm grows white, mid-blue, and deep blue varieties.

Delphiniums are cherished for having a statuesque character that lends both drama and romance to gardens and floral arrangements. *Delphinium* is a diverse genus of about 250 species, found mainly in mountainous areas. The name delphinium comes from the Greek word *delphis* ("dolphin"), in reference to the dolphin-like flower shape of some species. It's fitting that delphiniums come in an ocean-blue range of petal colors. A hardy perennial, delphinium is short-lived, usually lasting two to three seasons. To ensure that their production is consistent all season long, Killing Frost Farm plants successions, staggering their growing areas with a mix of last year's reblooming plants and the new starts for the current season.

Based on personal experience, having designed wedding flowers and freelanced for area florists, Carly knows how precious blue flowers are, so she likes to grow a full spectrum of blue delphinium, from pale baby blue to navy blue, as well as white cultivars. At Killing Frost Farm, delphiniums bloom from June through early July, with a second flush of flowers emerging in September.

Because delphiniums do not ship well, they are a high-value crop. "They're one of the few flowers we can grow reliably," Jamie explains. "A bunch of white hybrid delphinium is so luxurious and fancy-looking

Below: Killing Frost Farm's delphiniums, in shades of blue and pristine white.

Above: The flower harvest is labor intensive and physically demanding, but the two care deeply about cutting their field crops at the perfect stage for the longest vase life. They know their flowers arrive at florists within one day of harvest, and that is the distinction that gives Killing Frost Farm a competitive edge in the marketplace.

for one of those six-figure Big Sky weddings, but brick-and-mortar flower shops also sell tons of it on standing orders. Florists appreciate the versatility of delphiniums. They can use 3-foot-tall delphiniums that have flowers all the way down the stem, but they can also strip off the bottom flowers and use the tips in shorter arrangements."

The flower stalk grows quite tall, so many farmers stake delphinium or use horizontal netting to support the stems. Jamie and Carly prefer the au natural option, despite their windy setting. "The belladonna gets this beautiful, whimsical curve in the tip of the stem, which is the plant's way of recovering from the wind," Jamie says. "It's a perfect, quirky shape that florists love."

WHEN TO PLANT
Establish new plants in the spring after the last frost. Delphiniums can be started from seed indoors 8–10 weeks before planting out. Direct-sow in early spring or early autumn.

WHERE TO BUY
It's possible to find perennial delphinium plants at garden centers for growing in the home garden. Carly and Jamie purchase rooted starts (or plugs) to get a jump on the season and save the labor of seeding them. Seed source:
   Johnny's Seeds, johnnyseeds.com
Plug source:
   Ball Seed, ballseed.com

"I never have a problem paying for plugs, especially for perennials like delphinium," Carly explains. "We get to cut [for] two cycles in a season and then the plant will bloom the following season. Plus, the plant might yield four to six stems from each plug."

HOW TO WATER
Water well throughout growing season. At Killing Frost, each row of flowers has drip irrigation tape that waters the plants overnight on a slow drip once a week.

WHEN TO HARVEST
Cut delphinium when one-fourth of the flowers are open. Jamie and Carly like to cut the stems at the base of the plant for maximum stem length.

Max Gill

MAX GILL DESIGN

The rise of farm-to-table dining is widely credited to Chez Panisse, Alice Waters's tiny Berkeley, California, bistro that opened in 1971 and launched a culinary revolution that continues today. It elevated the idea of using locally grown, seasonal ingredients. Chez Panisse's ethos has been adopted by subsequent generations of chefs, restaurants, and foodies. And from the start, Chez Panisse's floral displays have reflected their dedication to sourcing locally and sustainably.

Floral designer and educator Max Gill, owner of Max Gill Design in Oakland, has served as the florist in residence at Chez Panisse for nearly two decades, recently announcing his "retirement" to devote more time to his studio and design commissions. At Chez Panisse, he created several weekly floral arrangements, including large installations in the foyer and main dining room, as well as simpler ones for the upstairs bar. "The flowers have always been intended to enrich or accent, rather than compete with, the dining experience," he explains. "I wanted them to feel like a moment in time, representative of what you might experience during a moment in the garden or in nature." Over the years, Max regularly shared photos of the highly seasonal creations on social media, adding a caption: "This week at the Chez."

His weekly designs, exquisite but unfussy garden-inspired arrangements, were the impetus for expanding his floral studio as a full-time business. Prior to that, he bartended and freelanced for other floral designers, drawing influence from a degree in environmental science and his classical theater training.

Performing on the stage gave Max a distinct perspective about designing flowers for spaces and events. "For thousands of years, back to the Greeks and Romans, theater allowed people to determine how spatial relationships on stage could elicit an emotional response from the audience," Max explains. "Similarly, within an arrangement, there's a way that thinking in those terms, for me, enriches my work."

Today, Max operates from a 3,000-square-foot studio in Emeryville, California, having years ago moved out of a one-car garage at his former family home in Berkeley. There, he also developed an urban garden filled with orchard trees, perennials, and clematis vines—all of which supplied Max Gill Design's signature style.

Opposite: As a floral artist and designer, Max Gill is deeply rooted in the garden. Although he can't grow every flower his commissions require, he seeks out special ingredients, ephemeral botanicals, to grow in his Bay Area garden. When the stems and vines he clips from his garden appear in wedding bouquets, centerpieces, and installations, the designs reflect place, season, and character.

MAXGILLDESIGN.COM | @MAXGILLDESIGN

A time of transition occurred in 2023 when his family home was sold and Max began to sink roots into a new residence in Oakland's Maxwell Park neighborhood. He found the tiny 1904 Craftsman bungalow on a 13,000-square-foot lot after viewing more than one hundred properties. The garden was old but well loved, and it included plants he didn't necessarily want, like five banana trees, complete with ripe fruit.

Max is by no means a flower farmer or even a farmer-florist. He is a grower of cherished and unique botanicals, elements of which often appear as embellishments in wedding bouquets and centerpieces. "I've never cut exclusively from my garden for clients' events, but it's vital for me to have garden-grown elements for my designs," he says. "Every square foot of this garden is important to me, because I always plant like I'm making an arrangement."

Approaching floral design with the sensibility of a gardener also means that Max has developed relationships with Bay Area and northern California growers. "I want to rely on what's local and what's seasonal, but not necessarily what is commercially grown," he says. Wedding floral ingredients might be clipped from vines and flowering branches in Max's garden. Foraging, he points out, "really boils down to creating relationships with people who give you permission." The designer also buys from boutique growers, many of whom sell through Gather Flora, an online flower farmer collective with a physical location at the San Francisco Flower Market.

Drawing from the garden defines how he designs wedding and event commissions. "That's part of the joy of growing flowers and using what you grow in designs. It's interesting to watch the interaction between a plant and its environment. So, the struggle, the fight for life, reaching for the sun, how sister branches follow a similar growth pattern…if I can replicate that in an arrangement or composition, that's gratifying to me."

Opposite: Max Gill planted and tended to this Berkeley garden for years before moving to a new property and starting over. His signature style of layering plants to take advantage of every square inch of growing space is evident to anyone who arrives and ventures down the narrow path. *At right from top*: The velvety amethyst-hued petals of *Clematis* 'Jackmanii', *Clematis* 'Polish Spirit', and *Clematis viticella* 'Dark Eyes' in a mantel arrangement. Prolific vines of white-flowering *Clematis montana* var. *grandiflora* and *Clematis montana* var. *wilsonii* are paired with the branches from a hawthorn tree.

CLEMATIS
Clematis species and cultivars

Vines up to 6' or 8'
Shrub varieties up to 4'
Requires up to 6 hours full sun but prefers
    shaded roots
Keep roots regularly watered during the first
    two seasons until plant is established
Woody vine

FAVORITE VARIETIES
Clematis 'Cassis'
Clematis cirrhosa and its cultivars
Clematis montana and its cultivars
Clematis 'Purpurea Plena Elegans'
Clematis 'Romantika'
Clematis tangutica 'Golden Harvest' and 'My Angel'
Clematis terniflora (sweet autumn clematis)
Clematis viorna and its hybrids

The clematis is traditionally grown as a flowering vine in the landscape and trained on a trellis or through the branches of a woody shrub such as a lilac. When clematis is used as a cut flower, it is a precious and somewhat rare occurrence. The name comes from *klēma*, a classical Greek word meaning "vine" or "tendril." The *Clematis* genus, a member of the Ranunculus family, includes evergreen and deciduous forms.

Max grows an extensive collection of clematis, choosing favorite varieties for floral design. "But there are literally hundreds still to discover," he says. "I love that there's no end to the varieties—and I love that 'cousins will marry,' a quote from a gardener whose name I don't remember that refers to how readily clematis naturally hybridize. So new combinations are always happening!"

Clematis falls into the category of an "event floral," aka a special-occasion botanical. Growing them isn't difficult, but the gardener needs to put in the work of training and pruning for optimal blooms. They are highly valued for the sparkle and unexpected variety

Below: Single stems of graceful clematis vines are displayed in a cluster of bud vases.

Above: *Clematis* 'Jackmanii' and *Clematis* 'Polish Spirit' at various stages of growth.

Clematis collectors are familiar with the three classifications relating to its pruning needs. These can be summarized as *no pruning*, *light pruning*, and *hard pruning* requirements. The nursery tag will indicate the plant's pruning group. Pruning encourages reblooming, Max says. "They sort of grow to be cut. And the sooner I cut them, the sooner they start to generate their second flush of flowers." Cut clematis need to be hydrated in water, and Max often uses a postharvest hydration solution to extend their vase life.

WHEN TO PLANT
As it is a woody perennial vine, plant clematis as you would plant other hardy perennials, in fall or spring.

WHERE TO BUY
Clematis plants can be found at nurseries, specialty garden centers, and mail-order sources:
> *Bluestone Perennials, bluestoneperennials.com*
> *Spring Hill Nurseries, springhillnursery.com*
> *White Flower Farm, whiteflowerfarm.com*

HOW TO WATER
Water regularly and deeply. Clematis have deep roots.

WHEN TO HARVEST
Carefully cut clematis vines to the length you need for floral bouquets, arrangements, and installations. If the plant is supported by stakes or a trellis, you may need to carefully unwrap tendrils or vines in order to have single vines for your design work. When cutting vines, Max tries to leave as much foliage as possible on the plant so it can continue photosynthesis.

they bring a finished design. The best features come together on one long, wiry stem: buds, partially and fully opened blooms, lush green foliage, and delicate tendrils. When the flowers are finished blooming, fuzzy seedheads are formed, which are also valued for autumn arrangements. Clematis petal colors are highly diverse, in a palette spanning creamy white, celadon green, pale lavender, mauve, pink, purple-blue, and deep maroon. The flower forms may be single, with streaked, oval-shaped, or pointed single petals; little bell-shaped forms; or fluffy doubles with so many petals that the flowers resemble carnations.

Misty Vanderweele
ALL DAHLIA'D UP FLOWER FARM

Yes, you can grow gorgeous cut flowers in Alaska. Just ask Misty Vanderweele, who founded All Dahlia'd Up Flower Farm in 2013, her boutique flower farm in Palmer. In fact, being in Alaska has had a magical effect on the intense color palettes and robust health of Misty's blooms, as the short, 120-day growing season is enhanced by up to twenty-two hours of endless sunshine per day during the peak summer months.

Misty believes that sunshine fills the flowers with good medicine, as she has personally experienced their healing properties and witnessed the effects on her customers when they visit her farm.

She credits a potted dahlia seedling that her son Luke planted when he was in kindergarten for inspiring her dahlia obsession and providing a path for her personal healing. Luke battled Duchenne muscular dystrophy, and after he died at the age of twenty-one, offspring of that original plant became a lifeline for Misty and propelled her down the flower farming path. "It still touches my heart when I see a purple dahlia. I feel that there's a reason that flowers came into my life at such a heavy time," she says.

Sharing her flowers gave Misty a safe way to interact with others while grieving Luke's death. Initially, clipping from just a few plants in her Matanuska Valley garden, Misty sold bouquets at the Monday Market in downtown Palmer; then she graduated to the South Anchorage Farmers' Market, gaining a sizable following during the seven years she spent there. "That market created a hunger for my flowers—customers inhaled them and wanted more," she observes. The original dahlia patch grew from 54 inital plants to 2,300 plants today, and Misty now farms across a few fields beyond the family's log-sided house.

Her flowers thrive at the heart of Vanderweele Farm, a vegetable farm owned by the family of her husband, Glen Vanderweele, which manages 450 acres of vegetables and strawberry crops to supply grocery stores around the state. The time commitment of selling at the farmers' market, not to mention the forty-mile distance to Anchorage, prompted Misty to eventually leave that arena and devise ways to bring customers to her. She sells seasonal bouquets, dahlia arrangements, and mini-mason jar centerpieces at the Farm Store during her growing season.

All Dahlia'd Up provides a floral delivery service, too. When a friend told Misty she wanted to sign up for a "flower subscription,"

Opposite: Misty Vanderweele of Alaska's All Dahlia'd Up Flower Farm began with a small crop of dahlias, but she now grows an impressive list of floral ingredients for mixed bouquets and special farm-to-table events.

the flower share program was launched. Customers come to All Dahlia'd Up to pick up their bouquets as part of two eight-week spring and summer subscription packages. Starting in mid-May, the spring bouquets contain tulip, ranunculus, anemone, sweet pea, and stock. Summer subscriptions begin in mid-July, with dahlia, sunflower, snapdragon, yarrow, and other elements.

People who receive All Dahlia'd Up bouquets inevitably ask if they can visit the farm. Misty wants those folks to experience the uniqueness of an Alaska flower farm, and she's partnered with local chefs to design several events, leaning into "floral tourism" as part of her brand. Walking tours, a flower retreat, and Alaska-grown dinner tours take place under the watch of Pioneer Peak, a 6,000-foot mountain that serves as a picturesque backdrop for both marketing and guests' selfie photographs.

The farm dinner is Misty's marquee event, an immersive experience for thirty-two individuals who grab tickets when sales open early each year. People arrive in festive floral attire and enter the farm through a "tunnel" arch festooned with fragrant sweet pea vines. Local musicians entertain during a welcome reception on the lawn, and the group heads off with Misty or her daughter Jenna to walk through fields of summer annuals and rows planted with dahlias. They identify varieties and give guests a mini-lesson on growing methods. Before diners are seated at the 48-foot-long farm table, they join Misty and her flower team for a bouquet-making session. Guests place their mason jars, filled with dahlias, sweet peas, phlox, and delphiniums down the center of the table, and they admire the botanical spectacle while savoring the family-style meal. Late into the evening, with the Alaska summer sun still high in the sky, there's a sense of camaraderie among friends new and old. "I want my customers to feel connected to nature and reconnect with something they might have forgotten. I don't want this experience to be commercialized; I want it to be real," Misty explains.

The state of Alaska has gained a reputation for its peony farms, but few growers are as diversified as All Dahlia'd Up. Misty advocates for Alaska-grown flowers through her blog, on social media, and at speaking engagements at flower and garden shows. She also serves on the flower committee for her local chapter of the Alaska Farm Bureau. "There are something like four hundred flower farms in Alaska, and I believe our state has so much potential to grow farming here, not just with food, but with flowers." Occupying the role of floral ambassador suits her well.

Opposite: The purple dahlia is special to Misty, reminding her of the first dahlia seedling that her son Luke brought home to her when he was in kindergarten. An illustration of a purple dahlia now appears as the farm's logo. *Following spread, from top row, left to right*: (1) Field-grown dahlias thrive in long double rows, flourishing in Alaska's cool nights and sunny days. The plants are supported with a crisscross pattern of twine attached to 6-foot stakes. The sweet pea tunnel is a favorite feature at All Dahlia'd Up Flower Farm. (2) Due to the cool growing conditions, sweet peas can grow all summer long. Cutting stimulates more flowers to grow, so the vines that form the tunnel are always in bloom. (3) The dahlias are harvested when the flowers are fully opened, and are cut at the base of the plant to ensure it has a long stem. A pickup truck transports flowers from the field to the processing station. (4) Evening walking tours invite guests to enjoy the flower fields. (5) The one-hour tour is perfect for out-of-town guests and flower lovers alike. (6–7) All Dahlia'd Up's farm dinners offer a tour of the flower fields, a floral design session, and farm table to dining.

DAHLIA

Dahlia hybrids and cultivars

24"–48"
Full Sun
Heat tolerant
Requires a consistent supply of water in
    well-drained soil
Tuber grown as an annual or perennial

FAVORITE VARIETIES
Dahlia 'A La Mode', 'Clearview Peachy', 'Diva',
    'Labyrinth', 'Lifestyle', 'Linda's Baby', 'Pink
    Runner', and 'Wine-Eyed Jill'

Below: Dahlias can practically design themselves to create stunning collections for the vase.

Dahlias, long-blooming stars of the summer garden, are hardy perennials often grown as annuals. Their modified root system is a sweet potato-like tuberous root with an "eye" (growth point) at one end. The tubers should be lifted after the first frost in fall, overwintered indoors, and replanted in spring, unless your garden is in USDA growing zones 7–10 or equally temperate places. Dahlias are hardy in frost-free regions. They also can be grown from seed (available from specialty seed suppliers and nurseries) and from rooted cuttings.

The American Dahlia Society has organized modern dahlias into nineteen classifications by form, with added categories for size and color. Evocative descriptions—"pompons," "water lilies," "orchids," and "peonies," for example—hint at the floral shapes.

The dahlia hails from highland areas of Mexico and Central America. Centuries after cuttings of three species of the flower were brought by plant explorers to Spain, the parentage of tens of thousands of today's hybrids can likely be traced to those original plants, experts say. The dahlia is a member of the daisy family (Asteraceae). The tubers store nutrients and water underground and produce blooms on tall, leafy stems. Flowers are formed by petal-like ray florets, arranged around a center of disk florets.

Dahlias prefer full sun, ideally eight hours daily. Light, fertile, well-drained soil is best. For gardens

Above: Dahlias and their companion flowers, including the sentimental blue forget-me-not, another popular Alaska flower.

with heavy or clay-like soil, add organic material or grow dahlias in raised beds. Space tubers 18"–24" apart in holes 6"–8" deep and about 1' wide. Rest the tuber horizontally with its eye, if visible, pointing up. If you are planting from a container, place the root cluster with the stem facing up—about 6" below ground level. Cover with 2"–3" of soil.

Misty has adapted her growing methods to a short, cool growing season, but those conditions haven't slowed her down. For her climate, she relies on early-blooming varieties and prefers the tighter, ball-shaped forms. "They last longer in the vase than the dinner-plate dahlias," she notes.

There is one more secret to having the most flowers you can on each dahlia plant, and it's probably the hardest thing to do, Misty says. After the plant has four to five leaf sets, pinch it back to right above the third set of leaves. Use your fingers or clippers, she suggests. "What pinching back does is force the plant to send out more branches. New branches will soon sprout where you made the cut. And remember, more branches on the plant equal more blooms!"

WHEN TO PLANT

Plant tubers after last frost. To get a jumpstart on her shorter growing season, Misty starts her dahlia tubers indoors in pots under grow lights beginning in March, followed by transplanting outside on Memorial Day weekend. She plants in double rows, with tubers positioned in 6 to 8 inches deep holes, spaced approximately 12" apart. Individual dahlia plants can be stabilized by tying them to a 6-foot-tall wood or metal stake. Or stabilize an entire planting bed with a crisscross method, weaving twine diagonally in an X-pattern through each bed and attaching it to corner stakes.

WHERE TO BUY

Misty's favorite tuber sources:
>   *Arrowhead Dahlias, arrowheaddahlias.com*
>   *Dahlia Barn, dahliabarn.com*
>   *The Flower Hat, theflowerhat.com*
Further reference:
>   *Dahlia Addict, dahliaaddict.com*

HOW TO WATER

Water deeply every 3–4 days. In small garden areas, Misty uses soaker hoses. The larger growing areas are irrigated with a drip watering system.

WHEN TO HARVEST

Cut when the flower is fully open because, unlike many other flowers, dahlia buds do not continue to open when cut. Misty suggests cutting as far down the stem as possible (18"–20") for floral bouquets and arrangements. This step also forces the plant to keep sending up long stems.

Christian Ingalls

DAISY DUKES FLOWER FARM

Hawaii's botanical bounty is synonymous with lavish, brightly colored tropical blooms and glossy green fronds that resemble supersized houseplants. But the flowers that Christian Ingalls plants in tidy rows at Daisy Dukes Flower Farm on Hawaii's Big Island are more likely to resemble cutting garden varieties on the mainland.

Christian specializes in growing many annuals and perennials, including dahlias—nontropical varieties that are also called temperate flowers. To raise crops on a year-round basis, Christian takes full advantage of the microclimates at her family's fifteen-acre farm in Pāpaʻaloa on the island's wet northeastern rim, 1,300 feet above sea level. "We are in the rainiest city in the US, which means we get something like one hundred inches more than Seattle," she points out.

The property that's home to Daisy Dukes Flower Farm was a sugar cane farm decades ago. Part of the aftermath of that type of monoculture farming involves rampant invasives that threaten to consume the flower crops, including one nasty specimen called "guinea grass" by the locals. "It grows taller than me and has spikes that can pierce skin. There is no way that we could keep up with it if we did not use landscape fabric," Christian says. Openings in the landscape cloth allow each plant access to sunshine and precipitation, while the surrounding material suppresses weeds.

When she got started, Christian called her crops "mainland flowers" to differentiate from proteas, birds-of-paradise, and tropical ginger blooms found elsewhere in Hawaii. Her customers describe her bounty as "wildflowers." She now grows hundreds of varieties, specializing in the bouquet ingredients she once admired during her college years at Seattle's Pike Place Market farmer stalls. "We don't really have seasonality here on the Big Island, but we do have different day lengths and much different temperatures than the mainland has. So, we have to break the rules in order to grow flowers like dahlias, snapdragons, zinnias, sunflowers, and more."

Christian, trained as a marine biologist, came to the Big Island to work as an educator at Dolphin Quest. Since 2006, she has taught first grade at the Parker School, an independent K-12 school in Waimea, starting the year that her son Braedon was in her class. "I love teaching, but I also wanted to do something on this farm to share it with others." The acreage at the

Opposite: At Daisy Dukes Flower Farm, Christian Ingalls brings her positive outlook and deep connections to her community.

DAISYDUKESFLOWERFARM.COM | @DAISYDUKESFLOWERFARM

three-generational family compound "is our Cinderella farm," she explains of the semiwild property that has a flower farm at its center. "All of our animals roam free. We have a large pond with ducks. It's very utopic."

Until 2019, when she took an online course and started growing flowers in earnest, Christian didn't realize that florists in her area might have an appetite for local blooms, especially ones of the romantic, cottage garden–style variety. "I posted a couple of photos of little, wrapped bouquets on Instagram and things went viral—I kept hearing from florists who wanted to buy them, and I realized I could try growing flowers as a business."

Thanks to the rainfall and warm temperatures, nearly everything seems to grow at Daisy Dukes Flower Farm. "So many things here in Hawaii perennialize, even when they aren't true perennials," Christian observes. "For example, I have basil that lives on forever. And I can cut decent stems of my snapdragons for twelve months straight." She grows some varieties that do not ship well from mainland wholesalers and other bouquet ingredients, like eucalyptus and greenery in the myrtle family, whose import from outside the state is banned. "I have a florist on Oahu who will buy every stem of eucalyptus that I can send him," she says, noting that she can ship affordably via inter-island air cargo flights.

In December 2023, Christian opened Daisy Dukes Flower Market in Waimea, a busy town located along a major cross-island highway. The 600-square-foot retail shop gives her flowers heightened visibility and serves Daisy Dukes Flower Farm fans who couldn't easily make the forty-five-minute drive to her off-grid farm. The playful, feminine space is decorated with a tiki bar that serves as cashier counter. Like the menu at her favorite coffee shop, a large wall menu that Christian devised lists her seasonal designs, offered in small, medium, and large sizes. "Customers can choose the 'flavor' and the size they want, which we wrap as a market bouquet or arrange in a vase," she says. "There is also a living room–style seating area, complete with a pink velvet love seat and full-sized fireplace mantel, so people can envision how the design will look when they bring their flowers home." With a core team of designers who work at the store while Christian is teaching, Daisy Dukes Flower Farm is open six days a week. "I want our customers to feel part of the farm experience, whether they walk into the store or come to our farm for a workshop," she says.

Early in the day, Christian harvests flowers and drops them off at the Market before she arrives in her classroom. She frequently films Instagram Live farming updates for her customers, chatting conversationally about the flowers she's just picked, not to mention the ups and downs of her floral venture. "We know that farming is not always this wonderful, beautiful life," she admits. "Farming also has its dirty parts. But even in those moments, I find that just being able to work with the soil is a beautiful thing."

Previous spread: Dahlias are a highly favored locally grown flower, supplying retail customers and weddings designed by Christian and her team. This in-demand crop doesn't travel well from the mainland, creating a captive market for nearly every dahlia stem grown at the farm. Zinnias are easy-to-grow annuals that deliver big, colorful, long-lasting cut flowers to the vase. When grown with organic practices, they are equally important for culinary uses. They pack a punch when the flowers or petals are included in sweet and savory dishes and drinks. *Zinnia elegans* 'Benary's Giant Orange'. *Opposite*: By bringing Daisy Dukes flowers closer to retail shoppers, Christian has established a gathering place in her community where flower lovers are encouraged to explore their own creativity by shopping the flower bar or taking a workshop.

At left: The view across the pond focuses on the floral studio. This is a perfect spot for starting seeds and plants before they are moved to the fields.
Above from top: The Market is stocked with Daisy Dukes flowers, but also with accessories, gifts, and goods, inspired by a flower-filled lifestyle.

ZINNIA

Zinnia elegans, Zinnia haageana, hybrids and cultivars

12"–18"
Full Sun
Drought and heat tolerant
    (low to moderate water needs)
Annual

FAVORITE VARIETIES
Zinnia elegans 'Benary's Giant', 'Isabellina',
    'Little Flower Girl', Oklahoma
    series, Queeny series, 'Senorita'

Below: Zinnias deliver a big, colorful, long-lasting cut flower in the vase. When grown with organic practices, they are equally important for culinary uses. They pack a punch when the flowers or petals are included in sweet and savory dishes and drinks. Shown in photo: Zinnia elegans 'Queeny Red Lime'.

The humble zinnia has an illustrious history, migrating from its native Mexico and Central America to Europe in the 1700s, transported by a German botanist with the surname Zinn. The Aztecs are said to have called the flower "a plant that is hard on the eyes" because of its colorful blooms—in vibrant salmon, golden yellow, dark crimson, hot pink, and more.

The zinnia is one of the easiest-to-grow annuals, valued today for the same attributes that wowed the Aztecs: intensely colored petals in single or double forms. There are also cream and pastel varieties, thanks to recent breeding efforts from seed companies.

Zinnias are the eye candy that lure customers into farmers' market stalls, for the same reason that grocery stores put their floral departments near the entrance. Because zinnias are relatively heat tolerant, they are prolific at Daisy Dukes Flower Farm, growing for months on end as "cut-and-come-again" blooms that produce more flowers as they are harvested. "They are the little black dress of the flower farm, because they can dress up a bouquet, and I always use them when I need something special," Christian says.

Christian grows several varieties to cut for her floral customers, but one of the main reasons she loves zinnias is that their flower heads and petals are edible. She stumbled into the business potential of edible flowers after producing a bumper crop of zinnias that all bloomed at the same time. "The very first flower

Above: Field-grown zinnia plants span the landscape at Daisy Dukes Flower Farm, where the scene is graced by the appearance of a rainbow.

that emerges on a young zinnia plant can be snipped to decorate a cupcake," she observes. She markets organic edible blooms as an add-on for her wedding clients, reminding them that their cake flowers should coordinate with the ceremony's and the reception's floral palette.

The flower heads are sold without their stems, a great way to use what Christian calls "shorties" that may not be long-stemmed enough to sell to florists. "Every flower farmer has this issue," she maintains. Christian recommends that anyone who wishes to sell edible flowers should contact their state's Department of Agriculture or other relevant agency to determine requirements for handling, packaging, and marketing.

WHEN TO PLANT

Start zinnia seeds indoors in trays prior to the last frost. In Hawaii, Christian starts all of her seeds in seed trays, covering them lightly with soil and keeping the area moist until plants are established. To ensure the plants produce longer stems, pinch or snip away the first center zinnia bud, using the fingertips or a clean pair of scissors.

WHERE TO BUY

The zinnia plants found at garden centers and from big-box home stores are often treated with a growth regulator to keep them short and compact, so they may not produce the tall stems achieved by flower farms. This is one reason why growing zinnias from seed is recommended. Seeds are affordable and widely available from garden centers and online sources. Zinnia seeds are also relatively easy to collect and save from spent blooms. Here are some of Christian's favorite seed suppliers:

Botanical Interests, botanicalinterests.com
Johnny's Selected Seeds, johnnyseeds.com
Select Seeds, selectseeds.com

HOW TO HARVEST

Cut zinnias just before the blooms are completely open and when temperatures are cool, early or later in the day. Cut the stems as long as possible; strip off excess foliage and place in cool water. Zinnias prefer to be stored at room temperature rather than in a floral cooler.

Julio Freitas
THE FLOWER HAT

The flower-patterned baseball cap, a souvenir from a friend's trip abroad, gave Julio Freitas a polished look when he delivered masses of flowers to a wedding or event venue. The cap's frequent appearance in his Instagram selfies launched Julio's persona as "the guy in the flower hat," so when he rebranded his studio, it was an easy decision to name it "The Flower Hat."

Julio, a native of Brazil, came to Billings, Montana, to study business management. This led to a seven-year career in hotel management and hospitality, which provided an entry to floral design. "I was asked to decorate the hotel's Christmas trees and create silk florals for the lobby," he recalls. Later, the owner of Julio's favorite coffee shop agreed to let him design flowers for their displays, and his floral profession took off. Café customers asked if he designed weddings, and his calendar soon filled. "I was literally working around the clock and realized I would either have to quit flowers or quit the hotel." The lure of flowers prevailed.

That was more than a decade ago, and the shift to full-time floral design coincided with Julio's move to Bozeman, a resort and college town in western Montana. "I like to consider myself a florist-farmer, because floral design came first to me, while farming came out of necessity," he explains. As The Flower Hat's wedding and event business exploded, Julio no longer wanted to rely on flowers from afar. "Getting flowers to Montana is really hard. I remember one July 4th wedding when our order was delayed. I thought, 'There's got to be another way to do this,' so I started growing flowers that season."

The Flower Hat's one-acre parcel demonstrates the potential of small-scale growing, with six thousand dahlias and equal parts perennials and annuals, all of which supply destination Montana weddings scheduled between June and September. The Flower Hat also provides residential flowers for clients who maintain vacation homes at the famed Yellowstone Club, where The Flower Hat is the preferred florist. In the winter months, Julio and his team decorate homes with botanicals shipped direct from Holland or ordered from California farms, or they use their own dried flowers. "But of course, I love the summer jobs more, because we can use local flowers, and that's obviously the freshest thing that you can get," he says.

When Julio shifted from leased land to his one-acre microfarm, he invested in digging a well and adding electricity. He bought a small tractor, nicknamed Bruce Almighty ("He's little, but he can

Opposite: Julio Freitas farms on The Flower Hat's one-acre plot in Bozeman, Montana, where he grows annuals, perennials, and shrubs, and produces tubers and bulbs for his online store.

Opposite: Flower Hat University attracts florists and flower farmers who travel to Bozeman, Montana, to learn to grow, harvest, and design from Julio in person, with the flowers he grows. *Above from top*: The Flower Hat's workshops are designed to give students a combination of hands-on experience, such as designing a luxury floral installation using sustainable practices, as well as instruction on the studio's successful business model, which includes understanding proposals and pricing.

Top: *Sanguisorba officinalis* 'Morning Select' is a favorite variety of the plant commonly known as great burnet. Its blooms provide dramatic, deep burgundy contrast in color, texture, and form, often placed as small clusters for impact. *Second from top and above*: Julio looks for uncommon, seasonal flowers and herbs that give his floral designs an unpredictable appearance, including unique elements like wildflowers, berries, and seed heads. *Opposite*: The addition of a 20′ × 20′ greenhouse, which Julio helped to design, adds architectural interest to the farm and is often used for seed starting and nurturing tender plants.

accomplish quite a bit," Julio jokes). He also added perennials and shrubs to diversify his design palette, especially for weddings. The Flower Hat now grows a proliferation of hydrangeas—varieties include 'Limelight', 'Fire Light', and 'Quick Fire'.

The season begins with daffodils, which are harvested in time for Mother's Day, followed by tulips, peonies, irises, ranunculus, and anemones. Through the summer months, annual field crops flourish—wildflowers, zinnias, calendula, and phlox—and the season wraps up with a vibrant show of dahlias. The online store explodes with activity when The Flower Hat's spring dahlia tuber store launches. Julio only offers varieties that he's personally tested and found to pass his criteria as cut flowers. Julio has also added his favorite varieties of ranunculus and anemone corms to the shop for fall sales.

By sharing his floral journey on social media, Julio has developed a reputation as a generous teacher. "My model—being a farmer who also produces high-end weddings—is unique, and people wanted to know how to do it. Education is now a big portion of our business."

Flower Hat University began with in-person small-group workshops at Julio's farm. Online courses reach aspiring farmer-florists who can't afford to travel to Bozeman. Julio is expanding the online curriculum into a full-scale series that covers the process of growing a flower from seed and creating a centerpiece, including marketing a floral business.

Julio, creative and personable, is grateful for a hospitality background that informs today's floral enterprise. "Hospitality is what The Flower Hat is as a company," Julio says. "We want people to feel comfortable coming to us for questions, product, education, and floral design."

Julio believes The Flower Hat's loose, rustic, nature-inspired aesthetic tells an alluring story. "People want to know where these flowers come from, and the more local, the better. When I tell them I put that seed in the ground and I tended to that plant, and I can say, 'Here it is for you now,' they absolutely love it. It is a rewarding feeling to know I am growing flowers not only for myself, but also for others. When I connect those flowers to my story, I think that's really what ends up selling them."

SANGUISORBA

Sanguisorba officinalis
(common name, great burnet)

30"–36"
Part Shade to Full Sun
Prefers moderately fertile, moist, well-drained soil
Perennial

FAVORITE VARIETIES
Julio grows *Sanguisorba officinalis* 'Morning Select'.
   Other unique species and cultivars are available
   from specialty nurseries, including *Sanguisorba
   hakusanensis* 'Lilac Squirrel', *Sanguisorba menziesii*
   'Wake Up', and *Sanguisorba officinalis* 'Arnhem'.

Below: After receiving one *Sanguisorba* plant from a friend's mother, Julio has since begun to grow this perennial. To his delight, the plant is easy to propagate and hardy to his high desert gardening zone.

Depending on the variety, *Sanguisorba* blooms from early July through late September, meaning it has high value for florists. The plants' soft, oblong, catkin-like blooms dance above tall, wiry stems, and their burgundy-wine palette checks the boxes for wedding designs that call for sultry contrast to pastel and neutral flowers. Native to all parts of the temperate Northern Hemisphere, the plant was first grown for its medicinal properties. *S. officinalis*, specifically, is native to cooler regions of Asia, Europe, and North America.

   Julio first encountered this perennial cut flower when shopping in New York City's West 28th Street flower district. He was there to procure flowers for a wedding in upstate New York and had planned a burgundy, navy blue, and ivory floral recipe. "I had left some money in my budget, which is something that I teach my workshop students, because you never know what you're going to need that you weren't planning for," he explains. That's when the bottlebrush-like *Sanguisorba* blooms caught his eye. "I was attracted to the color and texture, and I bought four bunches, not knowing how I would use them." Later, when Julio was preparing for the wedding, the burgundy dahlias he had ordered began to shatter. "Any stem I could salvage went into the centerpieces, but I needed something else for the bouquets."

At left: There's a casual elegance to many of Montana's weddings, which are often held at lodge and ranch settings. The Flower Hat's design aesthetic relies on seasonal flowers and herbs, along with unique elements like wild-flowers, berries, and seed heads for bouquets and boutonnieres.

Sanguisorba stems saved the day, he says. "By them-selves, the single stems are wispy, but once I started bunching groups of them, the color was predominant. I tucked them everywhere to bring out the burgundy color. It's so funny how this one flower that wasn't even meant to be there all of a sudden relieved so much stress. Not having the color my client asked for could have gone really bad!"

Julio wasn't sure if he could grow the perennial in Bozeman, but since it is hardy in his growing zone, he wanted to try. A friend sent him a large plant speci-men, which he divided into eight smaller sections and planted in his drain field. "I covered them for extra protection and, sure enough, the next year they all came up and grew into beautiful, mature plants. They were almost 6 feet tall and created a cloud of the most charming little plumes of burgundy."

Because *Sanguisorba* self-sows, Julio has continued to collect seedlings to add to his plant collection. He encourages every farmer to grow this perennial. "If you're looking for bouquet ingredients, it's a great filler that adds such a wispy vibe to designs. It's great for boutonnieres because the stems are fibrous and they don't flop, even if they're out of water. It's not really prevalent in the cut flower world yet, but I'm deter-mined to make it a thing."

WHEN TO PLANT
This perennial can be planted in fall or spring.

WHERE TO BUY
Order *Sanguisorba officinalis* from specialty nurseries and garden centers. A variety of species and cultivars can be found at the following mail-order nurseries:
  Dancing Oaks Nursery and Garden,
    dancingoaks.com
  Digging Dog Nursery, diggingdog.com
  Secret Garden Growers, secretgardengrowers.com
Sanguisorba seeds are also available, but starting perennials from seed in spring can be tricky and requires patience (germination takes up to two months) and additional equipment (heat mats). Seeds are offered by:
  Redemption Seeds, redemptionseeds.com.

HOW TO WATER
Requires average water. Do not allow to dry out.

WHEN TO HARVEST
Harvest when the flower has fully formed. Julio prefers *Sanguisorba officinalis* because the catkin-like bloom holds its shape and doesn't fall apart like the flowers of other species. The seed heads hold their color for weeks and can be dried and used as an everlasting flower.

Diane Calhoun & Susannah Calhoun
CALHOUN FLOWER FARMS

The profile of a modern farmer is increasingly young, female, and sustainably minded. The mother-daughter team at Calhoun Flower Farms reflects generational changes occurring in New Mexico's agriculture families, as well as a changing environmental reality and changing consumer attitudes about where their flowers are grown.

Calhoun Flower Farms is owned by Diane Calhoun and her daughter Susannah Calhoun. Susannah's elder sister, Emily Calhoun James, started growing flowers nearly a decade ago, taking over some of their grandparents' garden beds in Las Cruces to supply her Albuquerque-based floral design studio. In 2015, along with their sister Lillian Calhoun, Diane and Susannah established Calhoun Flower Farms. The women grew cut flowers on a combination of leased and borrowed land for several seasons until 2018, when Diane and her husband, Sam Calhoun, purchased a pecan farm in the Mesilla Valley and devoted a few acres to growing Calhoun Flower Farms' crops.

Diane's agricultural journey began more than sixty years ago, as a child on her parents' central New Mexico ranch and 1907 homestead. As an adult, she worked professionally in university development and donor relations before joining Calhoun Farm Services, the family's pecan operation, and growing flowers with her daughters. "I come from generations of cattle ranchers, sheep farmers, and herders," she says.

"We all like flowers and, apparently, we like dirt," Susannah adds with a laugh. Yet, as one of the only flower farmers in southern New Mexico, she acknowledges that "convincing people that flowers can grow in the desert is still a challenge." The state's topography and climate ranges from one extreme to the other. "It's one of very few states that has all nine growing zones, and last year, we had forty-four continuous days that exceeded 100° Fahrenheit. So we know what can survive those conditions," she continues. Calhoun Flower Farms doesn't face water access challenges that some Southwest growers have, since it draws from the nearby Rio Grande River and also uses municipal water and well water.

Calhoun Flower Farms' reputation for luxury flowers and beautifully designed bouquets was influenced by Emily's wedding and event studio, Floriography. By working with Emily, the other women learned to elevate their desert-grown blooms for customers in southern New Mexico and El Paso, Texas, as well

Opposite: Diane Calhoun (center) with two of her daughters, Lillian (left) and Susannah (right). All three Calhoun women have farmed together, bringing local botanicals to communities in southern New Mexico and El Paso, Texas.

CALHOUNFLOWERFARMS.COM | @CALHOUNFLOWERFARMS

as surrounding communities. "We've done everything," Diane continues. "We've done retail, weddings and events, agritourism, selling wholesale to grocery and florists, and more."

They credit relationships with other wedding industry professionals with building a network that supports locally grown flowers. Calhoun Flower Farms also opened up their flower fields to area photographers in search of botanical backdrops for portraits and wedding images. "They have become some of our best educators," Susannah says. "When those photographers come into a bride's room, they know the flowers are ours because of the fragrance, even before they see the bouquet."

Flower farming has nurtured mother and daughters in very personal ways. Diane loves seeing the next generation of her family continue their relationship with the land. Susannah says flowers gave her a creative, healing outlet during a period of recovery from addiction. "I wanted to do anything to be with my family. As I was working on getting sober, this flower farm brought us together," she says.

Calhoun Flower Farms paused the planting of annuals in the summer of 2023, in order to replenish and rest the soil. At the same time, Lillian left the business to pursue other passions, and the family decided to reimagine Calhoun Flower Farms. "Our soil needed some work and we realized we will become better farmers in the long run by taking off one or two seasons," Diane explains. The process of restoration began with the addition of cover crops, with the goal of choking out a heavy infestation of bindweed and wild mustard. "Regenerative farming is the next step for many farms, including ours, because after all, we only have one layer of soil and we need to save it," Susannah adds.

Their six-and-one-half-acre parcel of field-grown cut flowers is located within the borders of the Calhoun family's eighteen-acre farm, which also includes three acres of pecan trees. Their

Opposite: An alfresco dinner in the marigold fields.
At right from top: John and Povy Bigbee (Nona and Papa), Diane's parents. At Calhoun Flower Farms, Diane continues their farming and ranching legacy, inspired by their lifelong love of New Mexico and its distinctive sense of place. A Calhoun Flower Farms–designed wedding bouquet features strawflowers, marigolds, sea holly, and the more conventional roses and chrysanthemums.

land is situated between two conventional farming operations where chile plants grow on one side and pest-controlled cotton is planted on the other side. "This situation and other factors have created a serious problem," Susannah says. "There is a great deal of tilling and seasonal high winds, and we didn't realize how that would magnify weed pressure. We were spending tens of thousands of dollars in labor to suppress the invasive weeds manually, rather than use chemicals. So that means we've had to take some losses, including digging up one acre of our lavender plants."

The perennials continue to bloom, and the remaining acre of relatively weed-free lavender is flourishing. "We're leaning into flower varieties that thrive in extreme weather," Diane says. "Lavender is a huge crop for us, but there's also eucalyptus, yarrow, celosia, marigold, and sunflowers. These floral varieties lead to an opportunity to educate consumers, as local flowers from the desert Southwest are much different than local flowers in other regions."

Diane gets emotional when she considers what Calhoun Flower Farms represents. "There are so few agricultural families and legacies left anymore. It's a blessing that we can still do this and that there's a younger generation coming up that is passionate. It's so affirming. I remember being out on horseback as a teenager, rounding up cattle. The beautiful vistas of canyons and those Georgia O'Keefe landscapes were all around me. And I remember thinking, 'This is what it means to be an environmentalist. This is about taking care of your land and making it the best it can be.' I hope others will continue to honor those of us in agriculture, because that's our whole goal—to steward the land."

Clockwise from top left: Flower fans of all ages love coming to you-pick sessions and the annual Harvest Party. An architectural bloom of cardoon (*Cynara cardunculus*), beautiful fresh or dried. As part of the farm's agritourism focus, the family has hosted tours, you-pick sessions, farm-to-table dinner gatherings, design workshops, and yoga sessions. Cut flowers, collected during a you-pick event and ready for a Calhoun Flower Farm customer to bring home.

LAVENDER

Lavandula species, hybrids, and cultivars

28″–40″ tall × 2′–5′ wide
Full Sun
Prefers well-drained soil but tolerates poor soil
Woody shrub

FAVORITE VARIETIES

Lavandula angustifolia 'Munstead' (English lavender, formerly *L. officinalis*), a petite plant that produces a perfect blend of aromas. These stems are short, perfect for sachets and other decorative uses.

Lavandula × *intermedia* 'Provence', with a beautiful deep purple color and fruity aroma, retains its dark hue when dried. This is a fast-growing variety.

Lavandula × *intermedia* 'Grosso' has an earthy, cinnamon aroma and the highest oil yield of all varieties. This variety requires the least amount of water.

Lavandula dentata (French lavender), commonly called "fringed" or "toothed" lavender for its serrated leaf margins. French lavender thrives in Zones 8 and warmer.

The romance of lavender is one of the joys of gardening and flower farming alike. Bees flock to the aromatic purple blooms, and humans are attracted to lavender's many sensory traits, including the heady fragrance released to the touch.

A woody evergreen perennial herb, lavender is valued for its silvery-gray foliage and long-blooming purple spikes. All this plant needs is well-drained soil and plenty of sunshine. As it is native to the Mediterranean region, lavender adapts to the hot, arid conditions of Calhoun Flower Farms' southwest New Mexico location.

It's typical to see row upon row of lavender in commercial growing operations. The Calhouns prefer to grow the plant in elevated beds to ensure good drainage not offered by their native clay soil.

Below: Lavender flourishes in the arid New Mexico landscape, where Calhoun Flower Farm has put an emphasis on growing the Mediterranean crop.

WHEN TO PLANT

Plant lavender in spring or fall. In their region, the Calhouns have the best results planting in early October (due to an average November 1st frost date) or in late April.

WHERE TO BUY

Many garden centers and specialty nurseries stock potted lavender plants from 4-inch to 2-gallon sizes. Starting lavender from seed is a long, slow endeavor, and Diane and Susannah do not recommend that approach. Many flower farmers order lavender plugs from reputable brokers, which is an economical way to plant a large area at once.

HOW TO WATER

Nurture seedlings with alternate-day waterings for the first 30–60 days. At that point, pinch the central leader (prominent stem) to encourage even foliage growth and shape.

WHEN TO HARVEST

Cut stems when the flower heads on the bottom third of the stem begin to separate from the stem. At Calhoun Flower Farm, this is typically around the summer solstice. Use a hand scythe for best results and place stems in a bucket of shallow, cool water. Store in a cool, dark place. Refrigeration is not needed.

At left from top: A refreshing citrus cocktail, garnished with a lavender wand. Muslin drawstring bags are filled with dried 'Grosso' lavender florets to create Calhoun Flower Farms' signature sachet product line.

Briana Bosch

BLOSSOM & BRANCH FARM

The idea of living a self-sufficient lifestyle and nurturing the land felt like a lifeline when Briana Bosch left her corporate career and professional ballet dancing behind. "I knew I wanted to farm. I knew I wanted my hands in the dirt. I knew it would be therapeutic for me, but I didn't want to grow corn or soybeans. Then I started finding out about flower farming and fell in love with the flowers and the land," she says.

With her husband, Dave Bosch, Briana made a rather sudden decision to buy their 1920s-era brick bungalow, with a fruit orchard and horse barn, after she saw the real estate listing. "This place was totally overrun with weeds when we first arrived," she says. "But now, we have one acre dedicated to production of cut flowers and just over one-half acre dedicated to habitat, which we let be wild to attract bird life and help with pest management."

With two toddlers in tow, Briana and Dave made the move here in 2019 after selling the suburban Denver home they had just renovated. Briana saw the property's potential and envisioned nurturing the land as a wild prairie meadow with native plants, but she also felt emotionally drawn there at a time when she was grieving the loss of a close friend.

Blossom & Branch's farm name refers to its unique, 1.7-acre terrain, roughly divided between field flowers (annuals, roses, and peonies), and a woodland area where Briana and Dave have planted dozens of American plum trees and native shrubs (chokecherries, currants, and serviceberries) to encourage a habitat for wildlife and pollinators. The property is located fifteen minutes west of Denver, close to the foothills and close to the city. "We are fairly urban here; we actually have seven neighbors surrounding the property," she notes.

These days, gardening, growing, and floral design workshops take place inside a former horse barn, restored using reclaimed materials and architectural salvage. Dried lavender bunches hang between the ceiling beams. A woodburning stove warms the inside during holiday wreath-making classes where students gather at a farm table fashioned from old fencing. When the weather improves, Briana rolls open the large sliding doors to set up workshop tables outside. "There's definitely that farmhouse aesthetic here," she says.

The barn is also a film studio where Briana frequently records mini-lessons to share gardening, growing, and sustainability practices, posting to her farm's YouTube channel and to

Opposite: Briana Bosch integrates her sustainable values into all aspects of Blossom & Branch, an urban flower farm located outside of Denver.

BLOSSOMANDBRANCHFARM.COM | @BLOSSOMANDBRANCHFARM

Instagram. She also hosts video courses on regenerative farming and floral design geared to the home gardener. "A lot of the practices I use are closer to what someone would use in their garden, rather than on a farm. For example, we have a lot of flowers, but I'm not using a tractor; I'm using a broadfork tool. Teaching our methods to the home gardener can have a big impact when it comes to climate change and reducing the bagged and bottled products they buy and throw away—farming informs all of it."

Briana encourages local customers to shop at Blossom & Branch's farm stand, which she stocks with premade bouquets. "I wanted to differentiate from a farmers' market by saying, 'Hey, you can actually come and see where these flowers are being grown, and you can meet and talk to the farmer who grows them.' We've developed a community that rallies around us, and our local customers are very supportive."

The other main outlets for Blossom & Branch's crops include providing flowers for a few weddings that she designs herself and selling flowers to a small group of area florists. "We want to work with florists who share our sustainability values, people who don't use floral foam and who are dedicated to finding alternatives to invasive plants." Those florists appreciate Briana's seasonally driven aesthetic. "It's great when they come to me and ask, 'What's looking good this week?' Instead of me trying to hold a specific flower in the cooler for someone who needs it in three weeks, I would rather have the freedom and flexibility to provide the best, freshest flowers."

It all circles back to the idea of regeneration that prompted the family's shift in lifestyle. "One of the main reasons we wanted to move to a farm was to give our girls the opportunity to run around and explore. We think it's so important for kids to observe nature in an unguided way, to find, and learn, and touch, and experience," Briana explains. She would love to eventually farm less and spend more time caring for the native plantings, while also using Blossom & Branch as her home base for educational projects. "We're converting more of this land with native plants; I think we are growing at least fifty percent native plants and thirty percent perennials. That means we use less water and provide more pollinator habitat. I don't harvest everything, because I try and leave as much as possible to feed the pollinators."

Previous spread: The Bosch family has turned a neglected property into a bountiful and beautiful homestead, with the goal of eventually growing more native plants for pollinators, wildlife, and habitat. *Opposite, clockwise from top*: An aging horse barn was relocated to the cutting garden. Briana and Dave used reclaimed materials to install a new floor and added recycled windows and sliding barn doors. The inviting interior is furnished with an antique sink, shelving, and a worktable built from used fencing and boards. The farm serves as an outdoor classroom for Briana's homeschooling of their two young daughters. "Our days may consist of making soil blocks and learning about seed germination, looking at soil under a microscope, or talking about the microbiome of seeds," she says.

YARROW

Achillea millefolium and cultivars

30″–36″
Full Sun
Drought and heat tolerant
  (low to moderate water needs)
Native perennial

FAVORITE VARIETIES
Achillea 'Firefly Peach Sky' and 'White Diamond'

Below: Briana is a big fan of yarrow. "Not only is it beautiful, it's also heat and drought tolerant," she says. "It really is a bulletproof plant." She points out that while native yarrow is usually white or yellow (and is best for pollinators), the cultivars come in a range of colors, including reds, pinks, and peaches.

Yarrow's flat-topped blooms are actually clusters of tiny florets, radiating a cottage garden charm. Upward-facing blooms stand erect on strong stems that have aromatic gray-green foliage. The fernlike leaves complement pastel and bright-colored flower heads and add texture when used in floral arrangements. Yarrow's umbel-shaped flowers develop 2″ to 4″ across. When open, the numerous florets show off bright contrasting pin-dot centers.

Yarrow is native to all temperate regions of the Northern Hemisphere. The *Achillea* genus was named by Linnaeus in 1753, when he also named the species *Achillea millefolium*, from specimens collected in Europe. Achilles of Greek mythology is believed to have discovered the medicinal uses of this plant for healing wounds. *Millefolium* means "a thousand leaves."

Briana values yarrow for its many features. In addition to its drought-tolerant properties, yarrow is a food source for pollinators in the garden. Its long harvest period means that yarrow can be used all summer long for floral arrangements. At the end of the season, Briana cuts yarrow stems to hang for drying or lets the flowers dry in her fields. "It's such an easy perennial."

While she appreciates the true native form of the genus *Achillea millefolium*, Briana also likes its propagated cultivars, especially for floral design and large-scale floral installations like the floating "cloud" she installed above the workshop table in her studio. Cultivars have been bred into a range of hues, from pale pink and apricot to deep fuchsia and paprika red.

Above: In late summer, at the end of the growing season, Briana harvested all of her excess yarrow to create a floating "cloud" to suspend from the barn's rafters as a botanical installation. "The coolest part of this piece was that it dried in place—dried flowers are really such a versatile way to use flowers when fresh ones aren't in season, but they can also make a beautiful permanent piece of art," she says. To create this piece, Briana harvested yarrow with fully open blooms and inserted hundreds of stems into a length of chicken wire attached to the ceiling beams. The flowers dried in place to create a perfect late-summer homage to a favorite bloom.

WHEN TO PLANT

Yarrow can be planted in fall or spring.

WHERE TO BUY

Common yarrow (*Achillea millefolium*) can be purchased from specialty nurseries and garden centers. A variety of species and cultivars can be found at the following mail-order nurseries:

> *Annie's Annuals, anniesannuals.com*
> *High Country Gardens, highcountrygardens.com*
> *White Flower Farm, whiteflowerfarm.com*

Starting yarrow from seed is easier than it is for many other perennials. "Yarrow happens to be one of those perennials that is pretty easy to start from seed," Briana says. There are many cultivars of the native species, so if you desire a true native, shop for seeds from a reputable source. Seeds are offered by:

> *Everwilde Farms Inc., everwilde.com*
> *Prairie Restorations Inc., prairieresto.com*

HOW TO WATER

Water regularly until yarrow is established. Unless there is an extended dry period, you won't need to provide additional irrigation.

WHEN TO HARVEST

Yarrow blooms hold on the plant longer than many perennials. Harvest when the flowers have fully formed. The seed heads hold their color for weeks and can be dried and used as an everlasting flower.

the FLOWER FARMERS

Northwest

Bethany & Charles Little
CHARLES LITTLE & CO.

Bethany Dougher first visited Charles Little & Co. in 1994, after reading a story in the local newspaper about Charles and his flowers. Founded more than thirty years ago in Oregon's Willamette Valley on land endowed with rich riverbed soil, the farm was originally known as a major grower of dried flowers for the floral and craft marketplace.

A native Oregonian, gardener, and dried flower artist with farming aspirations, Bethany arrived at Charles Little & Co. in pursuit of double-flowering larkspur for her design projects. She was taken by Charles and his "larkspur forest," more than four acres planted in every petal hue from white, to pink, to dark purple.

"I asked him for a job the day I met him," she recalls. Soon, the two were a couple; they married in 1998. They have nurtured the farm together, stretching one another's complementary talents as entrepreneurs who share a plant obsession.

They run their dynamic forty-acre farm as a team, with the goal of always innovating. Charles describes his farming path: horticulture studies in college, followed by two years of biodynamic and French intensive farming in Northern California. He moved to Eugene in 1981 to pursue a farm-based life on the land. "Initially, my idea was to find a place I would love to live and start a farm, and

then to find something to grow," Charles explains of the original quarter acre where he got his start. Initially, growing flowers that could be dried appealed to him because of their long shelf life.

There were years when he farmed seventeen-hour days. "I would be out there before daybreak—my morning ritual was to roll out of bed and go straight to work," he recalls. He was entirely self-financed. Charles poured earnings back into the farm, building a magnificent, Dutch-style barn, which is now its architectural focal point. (Sales of pennyroyal, a type of mint, paid for the barn, he says). Thousands of botanicals now hang in bunches from rafters in the barn's upper stories, where the dark, dry, warm climate is perfect for the task.

Trends are often cyclical, especially in the floral marketplace. Charles is delighted that dried flowers are again fashionable. He points out that fresh flower wholesalers who in the past had no interest in stocking dried flowers are now ordering large quantities, thanks to increasing customer demand. One difference between the dried statice, goldenrod, celosia, and lamb's ears of old and today's dried flower palette is the explosion of botanical choices—even premium blooms like peonies and dahlias are sold as dried flowers.

Opposite: Charles and Bethany Little, partners in life and in flower farming, at Charles Little & Co., in Eugene, Oregon.

CHARLESLITTLEANDCOMPANY.COM | @CHARLESLITTLEANDCO

Opposite: There is a painterly quality to the view of this section of perennials, which is fitting because Charles Little & Co. is open to artists and photographers, as well as birders and other nature enthusiasts, who frequently visit to experience the pastoral setting.
Above from top: Three stories tall, the big barn stands at the heart of operations, its unique architectural outline defined against the Oregon sky. When Charles designed the barn, he drove around Lane County, looking for old barns to inspire him. Monthly Harvest & Design workshops, led by Bethany, teach students about flower-growing as they tour the fields to cut their own stems and later make an arrangement.

In addition to growing numerous varieties of flowers for drying, Bethany and Charles have built a national reputation as growers of fresh-cut annuals, perennials, and foliage, including branches harvested from acres of trees and shrubs. Woody ornamental branches, valued for their diverse features (buds, flowers, pods, and foliage), check a lot of boxes for Charles. "I want to grow plants that can be sold at multiple stages," he points out.

As caretakers of property they deeply cherish, Bethany and Charles value its ecosystem. Their land is home to plants, pollinators, birds, wildlife, and wild edibles like morel mushrooms. They walk along the rows of flowers that travel between their fields and the banks of the Willamette River's Coast Fork, observing the changing seasons and the grand view of Mount Pisgah. They welcome farm stand shoppers who come to pick flowers or buy bouquets each week from May through December, and they host students who follow Bethany on field tours before taking a lesson from her.

Well aware of the farm's amazing history, Charles has an eye on the future. "It occurred to me recently that my farming life has come full circle since 1986, when I was determined to make a living selling flowers that I grew and dried. Now, what gets me most excited about our future is—once again—dried flower farming," Charles says.

With a soaring, Dutch-style roofline, the loft has ample space for thousands of flower bunches to undergo the slow, dry, and dark drying process. The bunches span the loft to create their own beautiful tapestry, which frames Bethany at her worktable.

DRIED FLOWERS

TEN BEST ANNUAL FLOWERS TO DRY

Amaranth (*Amaranthus caudatus; A. cruentus*)

Ammobium or winged everlasting (*Ammobium alatum*)

Celosia argentea cultivars

Larkspur (*Delphinium ajacis* or *Consolida ajacis*)

Lepidium or Virginia pepperweed (*Lepidium virginicum*)

Nigella or love-in-a-mist (*Nigella damascena*)

Setaria viridis (or any grasses or grains)

Statice (*Limonium sinuatum*)

Shirley poppy (*Papaver rhoeas*)

Strawflower (*Xerochrysum bracteatum*)

Renewed interest in dried flowers has inspired florists interested in sustainable sourcing practices and growers eager to extend their season beyond the first frost of autumn. A visit to Charles Little & Co., in Eugene, Oregon, reveals an almost endless variety of everlastings–everything from Ammobium (also known as "winged everlasting," with tiny daisy-like flowers) to yarrow (with its flat-topped, umbel form) hangs from the rafters inside their magnificent barn, a satisfying array of cut flowers that provides beauty long after they've been harvested. *Echinops*, or globe thistle, is a bestseller, valued for its modern, orb-like form and its intense blue hue, even when dried.

According to Bethany, it's okay to combine dried and fresh stems in water when used for event work such as wedding centerpieces or a bridal bouquet. Otherwise, insert the dried flowers with stems cut short enough to not touch the vase water of a fresh flower arrangement.

There is nothing more sustainable than finding a new use for a flower that you may have in excess, Charles points out. Once dried, it's no longer as perishable, appealing to designers who want to produce a swag, spray, or wreath and not worry about its shelf life.

Below: This accordion-style drying rack is ideal for processing smaller batches of annuals, which are hung upside down until the moisture evaporates from flower heads and stems. The varieties here include strawflower, celosia, and statice.

WHEN TO HARVEST

Bethany points out that it's possible to dry any fresh flower, but certain ones are better suited to the process. The harvest stage for drying varies depending on the plant, so the grower will need to experiment with what is ideal for each flower. One tip: If you let your flower bloom to its absolute mature stage, it's probably too old to dry and will likely shatter during the process.

HOW TO DRY

Naturally dried botanicals require heat, good air circulation, and time. Gather fresh flowers into tied bunches and hang them upside down for three to six weeks until dry.

PRESERVE COLORFASTNESS

Eventually, all dried flowers will fade, but drying them in the dark ensures longer-lasting pigments. Store dried floral inventory in a box, away from sunlight and in a bug-free environment.

At left from top: A harvest basket and ceramic urn stand on a workbench, collecting pinecones, buds, pods, and seedheads—all gathered from the grounds and used to embellish the wreaths sold at Charles Little & Co.'s farm stand. Charles holds bunches of strawflowers. It's one of the farm's most popular crops, sold in the summer months as a fresh flower and then, later in the fall and winter, as a dried flower.

Rizaniño "Riz" Reyes
RHR HORTICULTURE

His personal tagline, "to live a life surrounded by plants and flowers," is an enduring philosophy that began for Rizaniño "Riz" Reyes as a young boy growing up on a fruit farm in the Philippines.

Today, "plantsman" is an apt description for Riz, but he is also a celebrated garden designer, floral designer, educator, and horticulture professional who has worked for public gardens and private clients and businesses in the Seattle area. In 2022, Riz authored a popular children's book called *GROW, A Family Guide to Plants and How to Grow Them*. His work is rooted in the wild and cultivated environment, as he draws inspiration from nature's intricate fragments, textures, and scents.

Riz established RHR Horticulture more than twenty years ago, first as a hobby specialty nursery propagating rare and unusual plants that he collected; it then evolved into garden design and consultation projects. He currently works in public horticulture but continues to be tapped for his flower-growing knowledge and floral design talents. Much of his volunteer time is devoted to the University of Washington Farm, a student-run food-and-flower farm adjacent to the Union Bay Natural Area. Riz has deep ties to this place, as he graduated from UW with a degree in environmental horticulture and urban forestry and later started his career at the college's Center for Urban Horticulture, part of the UW Botanic Gardens.

"I actually got into horticulture through flowers," he says. "From an early age I wanted to learn the names of different types of flowers that I saw, either in the grocery store or in my neighborhood. I also recognized that connection people have when someone is given a flower—it felt like a pleasant and beautiful endeavor to take part in." After emigrating from the Philippines to the Seattle area with his family when he was seven years old, Riz was befriended by the woman who would become his first floral mentor, Cora Slechter. "She was the first Filipino that I ever met who understood the science of horticulture, and she noticed my enthusiasm for growing plants right away," Riz recalls. Cora shared one of her dahlia beds and encouraged him to experiment, so he planted lilies, dahlias, and various annuals and perennials and later entered Seattle Dahlia Society's junior division floral design competition, which he easily won. He was still in middle school.

"I was the type of weird young teenage boy who would spend his allowance buying flowers and plants for himself," he confides. "I learned as much as I could by reading books, watching

Opposite: Rizaniño "Riz" Reyes, owner of Seattle-based RHR Horticulture, explores the Union Bay Natural Area, a public wildlife area, natural restoration laboratory, and an important habitat next to Lake Washington.

RHRHORTICULTURE.COM | @RHRHORTICULTURE

videos and tutorials, simply studying other people's work, and just 'playing' with discounted or discarded blooms to create things that people seemed to like."

Entering a science-based field of study (rather than floristry) satisfied his parents. "When I discovered that horticulture was about the science of growing plants as well as an art form, I found the perfect collaborative venue to really express what I love to do," he says.

Other plant mentors appeared in Riz's life, adults who noticed his rare talent for absorbing everything they taught him. When he was a senior at UW, he studied in China, which allowed Riz at age twenty-two to join an expedition there with famed plantsman Daniel J. Hinkley.

Riz studied with floral educators who taught design mechanics and encouraged him to explore design on his own terms. His aesthetic is plant-forward; he's just as likely to use leftovers from a pruning or planting project as he is to head to the floral wholesaler for more conventional ingredients. "Working in different gardens exposes me to all sorts of wonderful material to work with. When I gather clippings from the ground, it's just natural for me to turn the debris into an armature or a hand-tied bouquet, rather than tossing it into the compost pile."

His brand of floral design begins with an affection for the flowers and plants he grows and tends. "When I got serious about doing flowers, I discovered that I could tell a story with each design—it could be about where the plant came from, who gave

Previous spread: The gatherings from a day spent in nature include moss, wild rose hips, hellebore flowers, bark, and an array of twigs. *At right*: Adjacent to the University of Washington Farm, the Union Bay Natural Area is an uncultivated destination in the heart of the city, one cherished by walkers and bird-watchers. Riz considers the landscape here a source of inspiration for his work.

it to me, what garden it came from, who the breeder was. This is similar to my relationship with the gardens I love, the ones with really diverse plant materials, because each one [has] its own story."

Unless he's dressed up for a fancy occasion (such as attending a recent gala at an Asian Pacific history museum with an intricately designed botanical lapel attached to his jacket), Riz can be seen wearing a leather holster on his hip, its contents including a hori hori knife, pruners, and a small folded saw. These tools of the trade allow Riz to clip a wayward blossom, saw off a broken branch, or gently dig up a patch of moss. "It's almost automatic," he grins. "You know, I grab my tools and start deadheading or weeding!"

That's especially the case when he stops by the UW Farm and the nearby Union Bay Natural Area, where trails lead to the shore of Lake Washington. Wherever he has landed as a professional horticulturist, these places draw him back, providing the raw materials for his many design efforts. Riz's involvement with the student farm started in 2014 when Sarah Guerkink, its former manager, approached him about growing flowers there. He spearheaded the program and now works with Perry Acworth, current farm manager, as they teach students and the community about growing sustainable cut flowers to supply the local market.

"Being involved in the farm has allowed me to create work that is meaningful and also accessible. Maybe it can make a difference in people's lives by showing them the many connections to food and flora," Riz says. "I feel very fortunate being a gardener and a horticulturist. You know, I'm wealthy in that way. It's not a big money-making career, but what I have an abundance of, I want to share. We need more experiences where we create something with what we already have and express our gratitude for what nature has to offer."

Above: Like a jeweler working with precious gems, Riz pays close attention to the unique details of each botanical element as he composes his design. *Opposite*: Gathering twigs and branches downed by a storm, on a winter stroll through the Union Bay Natural Area.

GARDEN-GATHERED

RIZ'S FAVORITE PLANTS FOR NATURE-INSPIRED FLORAL DESIGN

Assorted moss species

Checkered lily (*Fritillaria meleagris*)

Eucalyptus for its foliage and peeling bark

Fatsia japonica for its seedheads

Holboellia spp., an evergreen vine

Lichen (*Usnea* spp.)

Love-in-a-mist (*Nigella damascena*) for its flowers, seed pods, and foliage

Orchids

Shield fern (*Polystichum* spp.)

Twig dogwood (*Cornus* spp.)

Below: Riz fashioned a garden-foraged spring posy composed of hellebore, fritillaria, brunnera, grape hyacinth, daffodils, rosemary, and daphne, for scent. Silver gray *Brachyglottis*, glossy *Polystichum* fern, and branches of flowering currant and bearberry hold the delicate flowers together.

Riz takes his cue from place and season, based on elements offered by the garden or wilder places. "There are certain aesthetics and styles that capture my attention, but many times, I just use what I have to work with," he explains. "I can't always describe why I'm drawn to a plant, but a lot of it is based on the sense that it feels right to me. I might have experienced the plant before, seen it on a hike or on a garden visit, but it's something that resonates with me. And there are times it just doesn't work and I have to find something else."

Arranging from nature and the garden can be gentle on the budget, Riz points out. "I look for really unique, intricate textures, and other details. Depending on how much time I have, I try to let the flower, let the stem, let the bud, and let the leaf speak for itself and honor it."

The designs are often "of the moment," so Riz doesn't worry too much about vase life. "Some pieces usually look okay when dried, too. It's inspiring to make a piece of work and then see its afterlife."

There are many ways to gather from nature, including the botanical pieces that fall in your own yard, or those that litter the sidewalks in your neighborhood. Riz suggests having a natural curiosity about nature, emulating the way children pick up twigs, leaves, and

Above: A bridal bouquet with classic hybrid tea roses and echeveria succulents as the focal flowers, combined with foraged garden textures that include deer fern, fatsia seed heads, heuchera (coral bells) flowers, dried *Brunia*, astilbe, sea holly, yarrow, and nigella.

pods when at play. He describes the process as developing a visual vocabulary.

In his role as a volunteer at UW Farm, Riz has formed relationships with gardeners and arborists employed at the UW Botanic Garden, and he asks them if he can rummage through clippings for his use. "This is a space I've known for years in my different horticultural capacities."

According to Riz, florists may find that foraged materials and "natural" designs can be difficult to offer to the casual consumer. "It can be challenging to streamline a composition where consistency is key especially when it comes to pricing a product. How do you determine the value of a product with materials that were practically gathered at no cost besides time spent gathering and processing?" Some florists will adhere to a pricing structure they establish themselves and give a value to each individual ingredient, but this is very time-consuming. Riz suggests using the simple formula of "time and materials," adding that some designers have a set price and work within a budget determined by both the designer and client. "This may not accurately determine and represent the exact value of each arrangement you create. It's up to the designer to decide how they want their work to be valued."

HOW TO SELECT MATERIAL

Gardeners are natural foragers, and Riz recommends you start with what you have available. Be respectful of your environment and harvest or forage with permission.

WHEN AND HOW TO HARVEST

Botanical ingredients change in appearance through the life cycle of a plant, whether it's a woody tree or shrub, an herbaceous perennial, or a quick-blooming annual. Gather or clip elements that appeal to the eye, collecting things that are already dried (such as cones, pods, or seed heads) to pair them with branches about to bloom or evergreen material. When you cut, use clean, sharp clippers and clip back down to a point of origin or the place where a side branch appears. The goal is to maintain a natural growth habit by making it look like you were never there. Follow Riz's practice of not cutting more than you need.

COMPOSE AND DESIGN

As you create with elements from nature, strive to highlight their unique textures and forms. As with any floral design, Riz says the first step is to establish a solid, penetrable base and structure using your collected materials. "This is where skills in weaving and basketry basics can really be beneficial," he explains. "As you create a framework to support additional ingredients such as focal flowers and foliage, the foundation can easily stand alone as a piece of natural art."

Gonzalo & Maria Ojeda
OJEDA FARMS

Florists in Seattle mark the seasons by the proliferation of blooms that appear at Ojeda Farms' displays for the Seattle Wholesale Growers Market. Member growers of the flower cooperative since it was founded in 2011, Gonzalo and Maria Ojeda are known for the unique, high-quality cut flowers they raise at Ojeda Farms. Their twenty-acre operation in Ethel, Washington, produces more than fifty botanical varieties each year, including Ojeda's famous peonies, ideal for weddings and Mother's Day gifting.

When Gonzalo was in his early twenties, he arrived in Washington state from his native Oaxaca, Mexico, where he was raised on his family's vegetable farm. He found work in agriculture, harvesting strawberries and raspberries on an Oregon farm. Within the year, he had returned to southwest Washington and began propagating ornamental plants for a commercial nursery that sold bare-root stock to landscapers and retail garden centers. He later met and married Maria, and in 2009, the two bought a ten-acre farm in Ethel, a rural community accessed via US Route 12, the main east-west highway along the southern perimeter of Mount Rainier. Today, passersby often pull off the highway to park and grab fresh floral bouquets or baskets of berries at the quaint Ojeda farm stand, paying on the honor system.

When Gonzalo and Maria acquired this property, they inherited former grazing pastures in need of improvement. After years of tending to the soil and farming sustainably, Ojeda Farms has expanded to twenty now-healthy acres. Viewed from above, the property resembles a beautiful quilt of colors, as field crops come into bloom, vigorous green perennials burst into flower, and a cluster of high tunnels dots the landscape. Plants that need extra protection from frost grow under the roofs of low caterpillar tunnels or inside ten unheated wood frame–and–plastic shelters measuring 30′ × 96′, which Gonzalo calls "cold frames."

Gonzalo was first inspired to grow perennials such as astilbes and daylilies, similar to those he raised for his nursery employer. After noticing that a few key crops sold out each season—like all the plants that had been imported from the Netherlands, so not easily restocked on short notice—he offered to grow extra inventory for the nursery. "It was something I did on the weekends," Gonzalo explains. Naturally, he experimented with other flowering perennials, but never thought of cut flowers as a potential source of income.

Opposite: Maria's bouquet-making talents require artistry and speed as she prepares a peony bouquet for the farmers' market stall.

And then he met Janet Foss of J. Foss Garden Flowers, an established cut flower farmer based in nearby Onalaska, Washington. "I was surprised when I saw this lady walking across the field toward me," Gonzalo recalls. "Someone had told her we were growing flowers and she wanted to meet us." It was Janet who encouraged Gonzalo and Maria to grow and sell cut flowers as a business venture. She introduced them to the other Seattle Wholesale Growers Market farmers, and they soon joined the floral cooperative as member-owners.

Today, the original peony population has expanded to fifty thousand plants, found growing in long rows of robust specimens that frame views to Mount Rainier in the north and to Mount Saint Helens in the south, two distinctive landmarks of the region. Ojeda Farms sells most of its flowers through two outlets—SWGM and the Olympia Farmers' Market, where Maria operates the flower stall four days each week between April and November. Having both wholesale (direct to florists) and retail (direct to consumers) channels helps balance the mix of what they harvest on any given week. Gonzalo and Maria confer with fellow growers about floral trends, working closely with the market staff to fulfill custom orders. After years of making round-trip, five-hour floral deliveries to the Seattle market each week, things changed when SWGM invested in a large truck and began to transport flowers for its member farms up and down the Interstate 5 corridor. While this is good news for the Ojeda crew, other farm demands seem to have absorbed the time saved.

"We often work at least sixteen-hour days, and things don't slow down until November," Gonzalo points out. Down time comes in the winter, when family trips often take place.

Bringing their flowers to the Olympia Farmers' Market, their second sales outlet, allows them to move excess inventory in colors and varieties that may not fill florists' orders earlier in the week. The Olympia Farmers' Market is a beloved destination in the state capital, where shoppers can buy growers' bunches and mixed bouquets from Maria and her helpers or select individual stems for a custom design. Maria's is a familiar face to customers, as she greets regulars who stop by each week to admire the diversity of blooms—from spring's daffodils to fall's dahlias.

The Ojeda family has built a future for their children—through flowers. Here, they have raised three sons, including Ricky, a young adult; and teenagers Fernando and Edgar; while developing Ojeda Farms as the family's livelihood.

When he drives across the farm, steering a golf cart along 4-foot-wide paths between the flower rows, Gonzalo stops to load the wagon bed with buckets of just-picked blooms. He expresses a quiet confidence and the physical strength of one who has farmed his entire life, from a young age. His weathered hands grip the wheel as he starts the engine. His grin spans the width of his face, as he observes his flowers in all directions. "I like looking back here and seeing the farm," he admits. "I'm really thankful for all the things that have happened to me. I'm happy to be here and I really enjoy what I do."

Previous spread: Just-harvested peonies are sometimes processed on the spot, their stems trimmed and stripped of excess foliage and piled into bouquets for loading into buckets. Gonzalo Ojeda pauses for a proud moment, surrounded by the peony harvest. *Opposite*: Ranunculus are another popular crop at Ojeda Farms, fulfilling the focal-flower role for florists and designers.

SWEET WILLIAM

Dianthus barbatus

6"–24"
Full Sun to Part Shade
Rich, well-drained soil
Perennial or annual

FAVORITE VARIETIES
Dianthus barbatus 'Electron mix', 'Purple white bicolor', 'Volcano mix'

Below: This stunning, purple-white sweet William variety is a reliable cool-season cut flower crop. The flowers are long-lasting in the vase and provide both bloom color and much-desired texture to bouquets.

A short-lived, cool-season perennial that is often grown as an annual, *Dianthus barbatus*, whose common name is sweet William, is the cutting garden cousin of the floral trade's standard carnation. *Dianthus barbatus* is native to Europe's mountains and to northeastern Asia. In the nursery trade, short-stemmed cultivars are called "pinks," and they are often planted in the front of borders or in rockeries. Cultivars of *Dianthus barbatus* produce stems long enough to be included in market bouquets or vase arrangements—and these are the varieties that flower farmers prefer to grow.

With a light fragrance reminiscent of the carnation's clove scent, sweet William produces similar stems and narrow, blue-green foliage. The 2- to 4½-inch-wide, five-petaled flowers have fringed margins and bloom in shades of red, purple, pink, and coral, as well as in bicolored forms.

Numerous stories hint at the origins of the flower's popular common name, sweet William, including those attributed to a number of historical English saints and conquerors and possibly to William Shakespeare. Another explanation for the name comes from the French *oeillet*, meaning both "carnation" and "little eye."

Cut flower farmers also grow the heirloom carnation, *Dianthus caryophyllus*, which blooms in summer and produces fluffy double flowers that are much more delicate than the commercially produced carnation. The "flowerless" types of *Dianthus barbatus* produce all-green blooms that look like fluffy pompoms and are useful as textural elements in design.

Above: Inside a high tunnel, sweet William flowers are ready for harvest.

WHEN TO PLANT

Sow seeds indoors or under cover, 6 to 8 weeks before last frost. Cool temperatures of 50°–55°F are required to keep the plants low growing and basal branching. Avoid warm temperatures in excess of 65°F, especially at night, which will produce soft growth. Direct-sow outdoors in early spring when a light frost is still possible. Seeds need light to sprout; do not cover.

WHERE TO BUY

To grow the long-stemmed *Dianthus barbatus* favored by flower farmers, source seeds from online sources and specialty nurseries. Mail-order sources:

American Meadows, americanmeadows.com
Johnny's Selected Seeds, johnnyseeds.com
Redemption Seeds, redemptionseeds.com
The Gardener's Workshop,
 thegardenersworkshop.com

HOW TO WATER

Water regularly until plants establish. Do not allow the soil to get soggy.

WHEN TO HARVEST

Harvest stages range from when at least three florets are open to when not more than one quarter of the florets are open. "Flowerless" types, such as 'Green Ball' and 'Green Trick', can be cut when one third of florets are open. This crop is highly ethylene sensitive and should not be stored with ethylene-producing produce. Expected vase life: 9–11 days.

Erin McMullen *&* Aaron Gaskey

RAIN DROP FARMS

Like many accomplished flower farmers, Erin McMullen and Aaron Gaskey began as food growers who discovered the economic benefits of raising cut flowers. Rain Drop Farms began as a family hobby and vacation fund, but after more than two decades developing their Philomath, Oregon–based farm venture, the couple has transitioned from selling mixed bouquets at farmers' markets to supplying professional wedding and event florists who shop at farmer-owned wholesale cooperatives in Portland and Seattle. "We have tried to stay fairly diversified as we've been conscientious about growing in-demand flowers," Aaron says. Erin agrees, describing Rain Drop Farms as a "boutique flower farm where we want to grow the highest quality products."

Rain Drop Farms is situated in the foothills of the Oregon Coast Range, outside of Corvallis, where Aaron and Erin grow an array of perennials and annuals, including garden roses and dahlias. While a diverse mix serves to provide their market with staples, the couple strives to find and grow unique floral crops that set them apart. Specialty foliages, such as Oregon-grown eucalyptus and scented geraniums, as well as more coveted items like lisianthus, delphinium, peonies, and sweet peas, help to keep florists interested and coming back for more.

A self-described plant nerd, Erin has a degree from Oregon State University in botany and environmental science. In 1998, after working at a nursery for three years, she was ready for a change and took a job at an organic vegetable farm. "I fell in love with being in the fields and selling at a bustling, vibrant farmers' market." It didn't take long before she told Aaron, "I think we should start a farm." They first grew peppers, tomatoes, squash, and beans on land shared with friends, taking their harvest to the Corvallis Farmers' Market. In 2002, they began to search for farmland of their own. "I'm sure that any beginning farmer will tell you that land is ridiculously hard to find; it's probably the biggest limiting factor in making your business successful," Erin explains. They saw the potential in a four-acre property in Philomath, a suburb of the busy college town of Corvallis. The hilly, once-logged patch, part of a bank foreclosure, had been overtaken by Scotch broom and blackberries and needed lots of tender loving care. Through sweat equity, they revitalized the land and, with help from Erin's father, remodeled the original house.

They had brought several hand-me-down dahlia tubers inherited from Aaron's grandmother when they moved to the new place, and the dazzling summer blooms became the foundation for what was to come. Erin soon had to reimagine the dream

Opposite: At Oregon's Rain Drop Farms, Erin MacMullen and Aaron Gaskey are creative growers who have transformed a farming side venture into a livelihood for their family of five.

of pretty flower beds and borders inspired by her horticultural roots and establish flower crops in functional, 100-foot-long rows. "As we transitioned to growing one hundred percent flowers, I had to give up my idea of an old English cottage garden designed by Gertrude Jekyll," she says.

Dahlia crops are now established on a fifteen-acre satellite farm, acreage that Erin and Aaron lease from a neighbor and hope to purchase in the future. They relocated eight hundred rose shrubs to the nearby site, fencing in almost a full acre of land to protect the roses from deer pressure. There are also now twelve greenhouses on the two properties, as well as a building with space for the cooler, production, processing, and employee use.

There's no need for Aaron and Erin to explain to local customers why they named the business Rain Drop Farms. "When we started selling at a farmers' market, we needed a name in order to have our own stall—and that's just what I put down when we signed up," Erin says. "The name stuck, and we love it. We know rain here in Oregon. In fact, we don't know what to do when it's one hundred degrees all summer. We would not want to live anywhere else."

Their family has grown, along with the flower fields, and now Aaron and Erin have two teenage sons, Emmitt and Cedric, and six-year-old Beatrice. The boys grew up helping to make change and interacting with farmers' market customers. Their little sister is happy to tag along after her parents on their daily rounds. Aaron left his off-farm job working for a food-distribution company during the pandemic and brought his transportation and logistical expertise to Rain Drop Farms. It was a long-held goal of his to farm full-time with Erin, and, although the move felt like a huge risk, it is one of the reasons why Rain Drop Farms has experienced steady growth.

What began as Erin's flower farming passion has become their family's livelihood and that of several essential year-round crew members. "We didn't become farmers to become business owners, but we've really matured at both roles," Aaron says. "It's been fascinating to learn the ins and outs of what makes our crops profitable."

Erin adds, "I still want it to be all about the plants, and I appreciate the benefits of having a partner who's fully invested in my passion. Though he is the levelheaded and pragmatic partner, Aaron sometimes turns his head to let me grow a couple of the varieties that I absolutely love, even though they aren't the most profitable crops!" Fortunately, most of Rain Drop Farms' flowers are top sellers and profitable, and they have developed a loyal fan base among Pacific Northwest floral customers who are invested in their success. "We believe that local flower farmers deserve a chance to thrive in a domestic marketplace," Erin says.

Previous spread: A rusty pickup truck provides transport from fields to processing station. The set of Aaron's posture reflects a man focused on his tasks, as he carries an armload of ornamental allium.
Opposite: The flowers of their labor: buckets filled with bunched flowers, ready for delivery.

ROSE
Rosa cultivars

3′–9′ high × 3′–6′ wide
Full to Part Sun
Consistent water required
Woody shrub

FAVORITE VARIETIES
Rosa 'Boscobel', 'Bliss Parfuma', 'Distant Drums',
　'Litchfield Angel', 'Princesse Charlene de Monaco',
　'Wollerton Old Hall'

Below: *Rosa* 'Boscobel', a coral-pink David Austin rose.

The rose is the most seductive of blooms associated with floral design, yet few North American flower farmers devote acreage to this popular flowering shrub.

The story behind the rapidly disappearing cohort of North American rose farms has ties to trade policy, energy costs, real estate prices, and, most glaringly, competition from the commercial cut rose industry in tropical countries. Flower farmers in the United States and Canada simply cannot compete on price alone, and there are only a handful of commercial rose growers left on the continent.

At the same time, florists have fallen in love with the romance of garden roses, and many unique hybrids that have been bred to resemble old-fashioned blooms. Highly valued for its fragrance, voluptuous, multipetaled form, and dreamy petal shades, ranging from creamy white to merlot red, the garden rose has opened up new possibilities for boutique flower farms like Rain Drop Farms. Traditionally, garden rose plants have been acquired by rosarians, collected by gardeners, and cherished by wedding florists. Now they are being added to small- and medium-scale flower farms.

"There's nothing like holding an armful of highly scented roses—straight off the plant—and being the first person to enjoy them," Erin says. "It's so special to find a perfect bud, cut it, smell it, and truly enjoy it." To grow roses as cut flowers takes special attention, as Erin and Aaron discovered when they were first asked to grow garden roses for the Seattle Wholesale

Growers Market eight years ago. "We're still discovering varieties we love, and we grow a collection of David Austin garden roses and some special hybrids," Erin explains. David Austin garden roses are not easy to buy wholesale, but they are widely available to home gardeners through retail nurseries, she notes. "The David Austin roses are vigorous and hearty; the blooms are so ethereal, not to mention disease resistant."

Of their few hybrid tea roses, 'Distant Drums' is a winning variety. "They produce blooms nonstop. It's pretty amazing how many blooms come from one plant." Another hybrid favorite is 'Princesse Charlene de Monaco', which has a lush pinky-peach color with gorgeous fragrance. "It is really productive and loves our climate," she notes. "We are definitely trying to keep up with the color trends, but also settle on some of the tried-and-true roses that will stand the test of time."

Roses require annual pruning to remove dead wood, increase air circulation, and encourage healthy growth and blooms. They are generally pruned in midwinter, before the buds begin to break in spring.

WHEN TO PLANT

Roses can be planted almost anytime, but spring and fall plantings are preferred. Choose a sunny location with loose, amended, well-drained soil. Their roots need access to oxygen, so heavy clay soil is not ideal. Site the plant away from foot traffic, as the soil can become compacted when walked on. Allow space between plants for air circulation to lower the chances of fungal and insect issues. Roses are heavy feeders and should be fertilized in the spring and again during the growing season. Alfalfa meal, along with organic or synthetic rose fertilizers, will give roses the boost they need to provide beautiful blooms all summer long.

WHERE TO BUY

Roses are available as potted nursery plants or as bare-root plants from specialty growers. For hard-to-find varieties, search the online sources like the American Rose Society (rose.org) and Canadian Rose Society (canadianrosesociety. org). Another great online source is Help Me Find (helpmefind.com/roses). Some of Erin and Aaron's favorite sources:

Heirloom Roses, heirloomroses.com
Menagerie Farm & Flower, menagerieflower.com
Rose Story Farm, rosestoryfarm.com
Star Roses and Plants, starrosesandplants.com
Weeks Roses, weeksroses.com

HOW TO WATER

Water regularly until plants are established and during dry spells. Roses need about 1″ of water weekly throughout the growing season (irrigation or rainfall). One or two deep waterings each week will encourage developing roots.

WHEN TO HARVEST

Cut roses in the cool part of the day; early morning is best. Make sure your clippers are clean and sharp. Select a rose that is beginning to unfold and that feels like a marshmallow when gently squeezed. If the flower has opened too much, pollinators may already have found their way inside. (Pollinated roses are triggered to set seed and will drop petals more quickly.) Aim for consistent stem length as you cut (commercial cut roses generally have stems that are 12″ or longer). Cut deeply into the plant just above a leaf node, thus allowing for long regrowth. Place rose stems into clean, cool water immediately to allow for best hydration. Using a hydrating solution of floral food will help prolong vase life and maintain petal color.

Vivian Larson
EVERYDAY FLOWERS

To some, the phrase "everyday flowers" implies ordinary or common. But the blooms grown by experienced flower farmer Vivian Larson are anything but. Her extraordinary crops supply some of the top floral studios and festoon luxury weddings around the Seattle region.

Vivian has grown flowers for more than three decades on her family acreage in Stanwood, Washington, perched high on a bluff that enjoys vistas of the Olympic Mountains to the west and Skagit Valley to the north. When her children were small and her husband, Jim Larson, a commercial fisherman, was away all summer, she sowed seeds of sunflowers and zinnias in the family vegetable patch to cut and sell five-dollar bouquets at a produce stand for extra cash. She soon gained a cult-like following among locals, and with weekenders who stopped to pick up flowers while driving to their vacation homes. Her bouquet designs were different from typical roadside stand flowers. "For customers in the country, my flowers were cutting edge. I had flowers that people had never seen before."

Vivian took it as a compliment when a customer referred to her selection as "everyday" blooms. "To me, it meant that people were familiar with the flowers—the sweet peas, zinnias, and dahlias I grew; the flowers that their grandma grew in her cutting garden." Snapdragons, ranunculus, tulips, daffodils, and dahlias are among the old-fashioned blooms whose new forms and colors Vivan finds exciting. "It's smart to keep my eye on the fashion world, on the color palettes people are using in their homes, and what brides are seeing, because they will want flower colors that complement those trends."

When she graduated to selling at area farmers' markets, wedding florists and do-it-yourself brides discovered Everyday Flowers and became part of her regular outlets. But Vivian had entrepreneurial ambitions to reach a wider customer base. In 2011, she joined with fifteen other Pacific Northwest flower farmers to establish a producers' cooperative called the Seattle Wholesale Growers Market. The success of this farmer-to-florist hub for local, sustainably grown floral crops propelled Everyday Flowers and its partner farms from Oregon and Washington to become better growers as they competed with the conventional wholesale channels for the business of the top floral customers.

Early- and late-season flowers, called "shoulder season crops," are an Everyday Flowers niche—from juicy double tulips,

Opposite: Vivian Larson holds an armload of 'Durango Bronze' chrysanthemums, whose reddish-copper flowers are ideal for autumn floral designs.

specialty daffodils, and multipetaled ranunculus in early spring to the jewel-toned heirloom chrysanthemums in late autumn. Vivian has further refined her crop mix in response to wedding and event florists, who often need hundreds of a single type or color of flower for an installation. For that reason, she explains, "the numbers of varieties that I'm growing is going down, but the quantities of what I grow are increasing."

Five high tunnels nurture the shoulder season crops. The big metal structures shelter the value-added blooms, protecting them from fall, winter, and spring rainfall and boosting inside temperatures to warm the soil by a few degrees. These semicontrolled growing environments have a Gothic roofline designed to break the wind that races across Vivian's farm from Skagit Bay.

Her influence in local floral agriculture is far-flung, as Vivian has trained, mentored, and employed many younger growers, but she doesn't romanticize the profession. "The fantasy is that you're out in the flower fields in your pretty, flowing skirt with a harvest basket. Reality is muddy knees and sunburned skin and hands that look older than they are."

Vivian often speaks about flower farming to students, garden clubs, and industry professionals. Yes, they might also be competitors, but Vivian isn't too concerned. "Every time someone new comes into the market, our slice of pie gets smaller. So, you just have to be able to pivot. That's what drives innovation. My point of view as a farmer is that I want to find something new. What's the next new form? What's the next new color?"

She continues, "There are days when I need to step back and remember that I was there once too. If I don't share the knowledge that I've gained in thirty years, what's the purpose of gaining it? My hope is that what I've learned could make a difference to someone on their flower farming journey."

Above: A seasonal arrangement designed by florist Alicia Schwede of Flirty Fleurs, a friend and customer of Everyday Flowers. The vase contains white anemones, pink butterfly ranunculus, salmon-colored 'Cloni PonPon Minerva' ranunculus, and grape Persian lily (*Fritillaria persica*), all grown by Vivian. *Opposite*: With a section of blush-pink *Ranunculus* 'Amandine Chamallow' in the foreground, one of the high tunnels explodes with flowers that are often called "the roses of spring.".

CHRYSANTHEMUM

Chrysanthemum cultivars

36"–40"
Full to Part Shade
Prefers a balanced mix of loamy soil
Perennial

FAVORITE VARIETIES
Chrysanthemum 'Anzac', 'Apricot Alexis', 'John Hughes',
'Heather James', and 'River City'.

Below: Up close, the petals of chrysanthemum
'Grandview Butterscotch' simply glow.

Gardeners and landscapers have long associated potted chrysanthemums, aka "mums," with fall patio decor, but the heirloom and specialty chrysanthemums that enthrall florists are a completely different plant. Cultivated for collectors and garden society enthusiasts, the uniquely formed spidery, quilled, and fancy cultivars and richly colored varieties of the past are enjoying a renaissance in the US cut flower marketplace.

Chrysanthemums are said to have been introduced into the United States at the beginning of the nineteenth century. The cultivar 'William Penn' was shown at the Pennsylvania Horticultural Society in 1841. This tender perennial plant has a lot to offer cut flower growers, principally because it is cold hardy after the first frost, outpacing dahlias, which quickly succumb when temperatures drop. "I like to say that chrysanthemums are the 'last hurrah' for a flowering crop," Vivian explains. "They are my top choice after dahlia season ends."

Vivian digs up mum plants each December, repotting them and moving them out of the high tunnel to a minimally heated greenhouse. In the spring, when the plants push out new growth, Vivian takes cuttings from each variety's "mother plant" to root for the next season.

She recommends cutting back the plant by mid-July to encourage branching. "Let's say the plant is eighteen inches tall by then, with lots of healthy stems. I'll cut it at least halfway back. Those stems will then elongate and produce much taller stems that are great cut flowers. Plus, you might get up to eight

Above from left: The multipetaled form
of *Chrysanthemum* 'Shanghai Red'.
These burnt orange 'Kelvin Mandarin'
chrysanthemums are ready to harvest.

or ten stems, whereas if you don't cut back, there are
only three stems per plant."

In chrysanthemum societies and for judged exhi-
bitions, growers often train plants to have a strong
single stem that produces a showcase bloom, sometimes measuring 4″ or larger across; these are achieved
by disbudding, or pinching back side buds. Florists'
tastes for multiple buds and different-sized blooms
have influenced today's chrysanthemum fashions.
For example, Vivian pinches out the center bud of her
plants to stimulate more side stems, each of which will
produce a proliferation of flowers. This method produces the spray form. "I think giving the florist more
options with their stems is smart, because they can
decide how they want to use the stems, foliage, and
flowers," she advises.

WHEN TO PLANT
Plant rooted cuttings or potted nursery
plants in spring after the last frost. An
application of all-around, well-balanced
fertilizer is useful at planting.

WHERE TO BUY
To find uncommon or specialty varieties,
shop mail-order nurseries that offer
rooted plugs. Local chrysanthemum societies
frequently hold plant sales where
the collectors' favorites might appear.
  King's Mum's LLC, kingsmums.com
  Wildrye Farm, wildryefarm.com
For commercial quantities:
  Ball Seed, ballseed.com

HOW TO WATER
Water consistently for maximum root growth.

WHEN TO HARVEST
Cut individual chrysanthemum sprays when
the center flower is fully open and side buds
are well colored.

Julie Rémy

FLEURIS ORCHARD & BLOOMS

After traveling the world as a humanitarian photographer, Julie Rémy settled on Vancouver Island in Canada's British Columbia, building a small floral design studio in the heart of an enchanted garden. A French Canadian raised in Montreal, Julie first came to the provincial capital of Victoria when she was in her twenties, on a language exchange through her job as an ocean mapper for the Canadian government. Later, she studied photography in Victoria, which led to more than a decade working across many continents for Doctors Without Borders. As a visual storyteller, she documented some of the most challenging crises around the globe.

Years into that career, Julie took a sabbatical and found herself sitting on a white sandy beach in the Andaman Islands, in India, gazing at the turquoise ocean, and asking, "What's next?" She was in her late thirties; as a type-1 diabetic with many allergies, she knew that a lifestyle change was probably necessary for her health. The scene reminded her of Tofino Beach at the Pacific Rim National Park Reserve on Vancouver Island and filled her with memories of living in Victoria as a young woman. "I didn't really know what I would find there, but I decided to move back. I could definitely feel that's where 'home' was for me."

There, she worked in communications and as a landscape gardener and met Dwight Durham, the man who introduced her to Glendenning Farm in 2016. "It took a while before he brought me to his family's farm, where he was living in a tiny house," she says of her now husband, a professional landscaper. "When I saw the potential of this overgrown orchard, I immediately realized there was so much we could create together and make it look and feel like a magical garden."

Today Julie and Dwight, along with Dwight's parents, are caretakers of this special place. Julie and Dwight live in a restored garage, her floral design studio occupies a 130-year-old cottage rebuilt from the farm's original home, and they continue to transform the gardens to accommodate more flower crops. With its existing orchard and forested slope, Glendenning Farm is not laid out for machined agriculture, but there are areas more suitable for growing rows of flowers—some in raised beds, in low tunnels, or in the high tunnel, which is ideal for delicate, early and late-season crops. Curvilinear pathways are edged in clusters of hellebores, astilbes, peonies, roses, and sweet peas; orchard trees are skirted with more ephemeral blooms. The branches of flowering trees and shrubs not only provide habitats for bird

Opposite: Farmer-florist Julie Rémy has transformed sections of a former vegetable garden into a prolific cutting garden. The dahlia patch is located just steps away from the tiny Fleuris studio, where everything from seed-starting to floral design projects takes place.

FLEURIS.CA | @FLEURISORCHARDANDBLOOMS

life and other pollinators before they produce an abundance of fruit but also appear in Julie's large-scale installations for elegant hotels, local restaurants, and private clients. This garden is truly her artistic muse.

The idea for Fleuris Orchard & Blooms, which Julie opened in 2020, began some years earlier with her in-laws' dahlia patch. "I started to make little bouquets for their farm stand and then realized I wanted more. I wanted to make lush, elegant installations and very detailed wearables in pleasing floral palettes."

As Dwight was busy caring for other people's gardens and Julie's in-laws were entering retirement, they offered Julie a little patch of land for flower growing. Fleuris is now known for a proliferation of ranunculus, an expanding dahlia collection, and well over three hundred varieties of cut flowers, including tulip, masterwort (*Astrantia*), astilbe, poppy, pincushion flower (*Scabiosa*), and more choices to round out the seasons. "As I started gardening, growing, and observing the seasons, I realized that what I am doing is beneficial for the land and people. If I can inspire just one person to open their eyes and observe the fleeting beauty of nature, and even grow a few flowers, that's what I want my efforts to achieve," Julie says.

Through her studio, Julie designs custom bouquets and arrangements, sells subscriptions, and leads workshops, drawing materials from the farm's mature woodland plantings and from her cut flower operation. She chooses to work with locally sourced botanicals, mainly her own, and occasionally sources from other Vancouver Island–based growers, emphasizing seasonality and foraging evergreens for holiday workshops and custom designs.

Access to the growing zones just steps beyond her studio adds a special element to Fleuris's workshops, which range from making seasonal hand-tied bouquets and sustainable centerpiece arrangements to tablescaping and wreath making. "It's amazing to walk in the garden with my students and invite them to observe the flowers before they start to design." She narrates their garden walks, often pausing to demonstrate the right stage to cut a flower or to notice the intricacies of its petal colors.

Today, it is flowers that connect Julie with the colors, lines, and shapes that once influenced her as a mapmaker and photographer. "Whether it's the ocean, the earth, or people—they all intrigue me," she confides. "I am simply a curious explorer who looks for beauty in our world and who loves color."

Opposite: Fleuris Orchard & Blooms is based in a rustic cottage rebuilt from the farm's 130-year-old original home. *Above*: Julie's design projects begin with cutting ingredients from the garden, or dried and foraged stems shaped into wearable botanical pieces or large-scale installation pieces.

ASTILBE

Astilbe hybrids and cultivars

24″–30″
Part Shade to Full Shade
Perennial

FAVORITE VARIETIES
Astilbe Arendsii Group 'Bridal Veil', 'Erika'

Below: Astilbe's soft, feathery plumes are a welcome addition to the forest landscape. They prefer to sink their roots under the dappled shade of a canopy of deciduous trees. As cut flowers, astilbes add a naturalistic, woodland aesthetic to Julie's floral designs.

Astilbe is native to mountain ravines and woodlands in Asia and North America and is known for its graceful plumes and lush foliage. It is a must-have perennial for designers and gardeners who have rich, moist, shaded areas in their gardens. Fresh-cut or dried, its feathery, textural flowers are useful in floral design. Attractive foliage and a subtle, sweet fragrance make astilbes quite versatile.

Its common names are "false spiraea" or "false goat's beard." The botanical name *Astilbe* comes from the Greek *a* (meaning "without") and *stilbe* ("brilliance"), belying the true elegance portrayed by thousands of miniscule flowers that form dramatic or feathery plumes born by tall, slender stems.

Astilbe is beloved for its ability to thrive in shady conditions. It adds elegance and texture to any landscape design, and its foliage creates a lush backdrop for its delicate flowers, making it an ideal choice around trees or alongside other shade-loving perennials. Astilbe's airy blooms come in shades of pink, white, red, and lavender, providing a soft, romantic touch to garden beds and floral arrangements.

WHEN TO PLANT

Plant bare-root astilbe or plants in spring or fall. Choose a location with moist, well-drained soil and partial shade. They will survive in full shade, but do best in partial shade.

WHERE TO BUY

Astilbe plants and rhizomes are available at nurseries and garden centers specializing in perennials. Some mail-order sources include:

Bluestone Perennials, bluestoneperennials.com
Longfield Gardens, longfield-gardens.com
White Flower Farm, whiteflowerfarm.com

HOW TO WATER

Keep the soil consistently moist, especially during dry periods. Water deeply to ensure thorough hydration, but avoid waterlogging the soil.

WHEN TO HARVEST

Astilbe blooms can be harvested when the flower spikes are fully developed but not yet fully open. Cut the stems at the base for use in floral arrangements.

At left: Julie tells her wedding clients that they can commemorate their nuptials with her elegantly designed florals while also respecting the environment. She chooses Fleuris-grown flowers and supports local flower farmers whose practices she values.

Tracy Yang & Nick Songsangcharntara
JARN CO. FLOWERS

Tracy Yang and Nick Songsangcharntara did not set out to become flower farmers, but they are now first-generation American entrepreneurs who operate JARN Co. Flowers and grow thousands of blooms for the Seattle marketplace. Both Tracy and Nick are children of parents who immigrated to the United States from Thailand. Nick was raised in Dallas and worked in his family's Asian restaurants while growing up. "The only gardening background I had before this was helping my dad grow in our backyard. I wanted to run away from the food service industry for a long time, but I never thought I'd be a farmer."

As a teen and young adult raised in St. Paul, Minnesota, in the sizeable Hmong community, Tracy competed and performed in hip-hop dancing, but she also was expected to weed, do gardening chores, and help her parents in their food garden. "My parents were avid vegetable farmers. We had a half-acre farm. As a child, I hated it," Tracy confides. "But look at me now!"

Today, the couple farms on a four-acre parcel of rented land in Monroe, Washington, north of Seattle. They specialize in high-value bulb flowers (tulips, daffodils, and dahlias) and perennial peonies, but they also raise plenty of annuals and foliage plants to round out their bouquet designs for weekly subscribers and farmers' market customers. They also sell seasonal crops to florists who shop at SnoCo. Flower Collective, a regional wholesale floral hub that Tracy founded in 2023 with several other growers. JARN Co.'s community-supported agriculture (CSA) subscription plan is a favorite way to connect with customers. "We ask them to invest in our flowers for the coming season—and in turn, they receive shares," Tracy explains. "We offer six-week subscriptions of mixed flowers, and we also have specific flower packages like tulips and dahlias."

JARN Co.'s home base is Tracy and Nick's townhouse in Everett, Washington, many rooms of which are filled with crates for forcing tulips and trays for starting seedlings under grow lights. To reach their fields, they make the daily thirty-minute drive in a truck filled with seedlings, usually accompanied by their two-year-old golden retriever–border collie mix, Donut.

Their farm's name, JARN, is inspired by the English romanization of the Thai word "จันทร์" which translates as "moon" and is also a root of Nick's surname. They were encouraged to start their own farm by Tracy's family, including her sister Laura Cha, who married into Va Cha Garden, an established flower farm

Opposite: Nick Songsangcharntara and Tracy Yang own JARN Co. Flowers in Monroe, Washington, located about thirty miles north of Seattle in Snohomish County. They lease acreage for their field-grown flowers, including bulbs, annuals, and perennials.

that sells at the Pike Place Market in Seattle, and Mama Yang, Tracy and Laura's mother, who often helps Laura during the busy farming season. "Farming with my mom gave me an important connection with my Hmong heritage, and I have absorbed much about my culture," Tracy says. "She has taught me about being Hmong-American and that our culture, the beliefs, the values, and the rituals, are all rooted in agriculture." Tracy, the youngest of seven children, now cherishes her mother's stories. "Mama Yang has grit and hustle in her DNA, I think. She tells stories about selling donuts on the street in Thailand when she was just five years old. No wonder hard work is kind of second nature to me."

In 2021, Nick and Tracy helped her sister during a Mother's Day flower sale—and Nick, an extrovert, was hooked. "It was the craziest time and everyone else was stressed out, but I thought it was fun," he recalls. Compared to working his day job in the automotive industry, being a floral entrepreneur appealed to Nick, and he urged Tracy to make the leap, telling her he was all in, too. She eventually agreed, and they started growing flowers part-time later that summer. "I never intended to grow flowers professionally, and I knew it wouldn't be easy, but Nick's enthusiasm made me reassess that option," Tracy says.

Nick says his management background translates well to flower farming. "On paper, I'm a data person, and I am used to managing teams. That's what has helped me organize our farmers' market stand and interact with CSA customers. I'm not looking at Excel sheets or sitting in on Zoom meetings. I'm actually working with people when I'm selling flowers. It's more human."

They value their relationships with bouquet subscribers and farmers' market shoppers. "Our in-person experiences reinforce the legacy we would like JARN Co. Flowers to leave behind," Tracy explains. "These are the people whose flower purchases impact our small business; when we're not at the market, they notice every time—and we hear from them." In addition to selling at four area farmers' markets, Nick and Tracy have developed other direct-to-consumer sales channels. They participate in pop-up sales at makers' markets and were invited to bring bouquets of spring tulips to sell at the five-day Northwest Flower & Garden Festival in February.

While intent on building JARN Co. into a successful farm business, for Nick and Tracy, the act of growing flowers is deeper than an entrepreneurial exercise. "I didn't think about my Hmong heritage for a long time," Tracy admits. "But working alongside my mom has been a full-circle moment for me. And I've realized that I'm right where I need to be."

Adds Nick, "This is not a spot that I think I would ever have been in my life before I met Tracy. But sitting here now, in this beautiful valley, surrounded by fields of flowers, I'm so glad I'm here."

Previous spread: The standard tulip produces a single or double cup-shaped flower at the tip of an erect stem. The bulb produces two or three thick, blue-green leaves that are clustered at the base. Tracy holds two tulip bulbs in her hand to illustrate the difference between a healthy bulb (left) and a bulb with some decay (right). *Opposite*: Rather than planting tulip bulbs in small batches, Nick and Tracy use a popular flower farm method to maximize space. Thousands of tulip bulbs are laid shoulder to shoulder in a long, wide trench that measures approximately 10″ deep × 24″ wide. Tulips are generally planted with the pointed tip facing upwards, but in this method, they often tilt over to their sides, which doesn't inhibit the direction of the stem growth.

TULIP

Tulipa hybrids and cultivars

12″–30″
Full Sun
Moderate to regular water
Bulb grown as an annual

FAVORITE VARIETIES

Tulipa 'Columbus' (Double Early), 'Queen
of Night' (Single Late), 'Renown Unique'
(Peony tulip), 'Van Eijk' (Darwin hybrid),
'World's Favorite' (Darwin hybrid)

Below: Premium tulip varieties are top sellers, and Tracy and Nick prefer to grow double and parrot varieties to sell as single-variety bunches or to incorporate into mixed market bouquets.

The tulip is an enduring flower of springtime, a symbol of the season's new growth that blooms at a time of year when humans crave the garden's promise of beauty to come. The native range of *Tulipa* is south-central and eastern Europe, the Mediterranean, and western and central Asia to Mongolia. The tulip's story is legendary, the subject of a historic period known as "tulip mania." That dramatic chapter of the tulip's past took place in the seventeenth century, when people spent small fortunes for a single bulb.

Fortunately for today's cut flower gardener and flower farmer, the price tag for tulip bulbs is now reasonable, and most of the very popular varieties are widely available. Tracy and Nick grow tulips in two ways. They plant twenty thousand bulbs in their open fields each fall, usually in mid to late October, tucking the smooth, golden-tan bulbs into trenches and covering them with a blanket of soil for the winter dormant period. But more recently, they have experimented with a method of hydroponic tulip production, which involves arranging the bulbs in pin trays filled with water, forcing their growth with heat and light, so the bulbs bloom as early as January.

Tulips range from early miniature species that grow in rock gardens much like their original habitat to late-season hybrids with stature and presence in the landscape, valued for their petal palettes. Tulips come in every color of the rainbow except for true

WHEN TO PLANT

Plant tulip bulbs in the fall before the ground freezes. These plants grow best in full sun, well-drained conditions. Rather than planting one bulb at a time in single holes, try the method used by flower farmers and dig a large hole or wide trench (approximately 6″ deep), and place tulip bulbs closely for impact when they bloom. Use a bulb fertilizer, water well, and apply 2″ of mulch to the planting area.

WHERE TO BUY

Most specialty nurseries and garden centers stock an attractive selection of tulip bulbs, available for purchase by late summer. Online sources offer collections, tulips in bulk, and uncommon varieties. Take note that most tulip varieties are categorized by early, mid, and late bloom times. All can be planted at the same time, but Tracy and Nick suggest that you select and plant varieties that mature at various points during the season to enjoy up to eight weeks of bloom color in the garden.

Tracy and Nick recommend the following sources for large-scale growers and flower farms:

A.D.R. Bulbs, Inc., adrbulbs.com
Ednie Flower Bulbs, ednieflowerbulb.com
Our American Roots, ouramericanroots.com
For small-scale growers and home gardeners:
Dutch Grown, dutchgrown.com
Johnny's Selected Seeds, johnnyseeds.com
John Scheepers, Inc., johnscheepers.com
Longfield Gardens, longfield-gardens.com
Roozengaarde, tulips.com

HOW TO WATER

After planting, water thoroughly, allowing moisture to soak down to bulb level. If autumn precipitation is late, the planting area may need supplemental water during dry spells. Keep the area watered until rains become regular, which may be as late as November. Winter and spring precipitation should supply sufficient water for hardy bulbs. In summer, the plants are dormant and require no water.

WHEN TO HARVEST

At JARN Co. Flowers, the tulips are harvested when the flower buds start to show color but are still mostly green. This allows Tracy and Nick to store cut flowers in their 40°F cooler for several days until taking their bunches to the farmers' market. In the cutting garden or landscape, harvest when at least three-quarters of the bud color appears. When harvesting, flower farmers pull the entire tulip stem with the bulb attached to maximize stem length. To perennialize tulips (so they rebloom the following year), cut the stem as low as possible to the ground, leaving behind the foliage and the bulb in the ground.

blue, with forms that include Parrot, French, double (with multiple layers of petals), and fringe varieties.

Home gardeners can allow their tulips to return in subsequent seasons, but most flower farmers plant new tulip bulbs each year to harvest more vigorous flowers. Over time in the garden, hybrid tulips will decline, and many homeowners find that squirrels and deer are the biggest threat to a tulip garden. Planting tulips in raised beds or tall containers can help.

For flower farmers and home gardeners alike, there is always the lure of new tulip bulbs to plant, harvest, cut, and arrange in our bouquets and vases—and the payoff of having a spring cutting garden filled with tulips can be had for minimal investment.

Diane Szukovathy & Dennis Westphall

JELLO MOLD FARM

Jello Mold Farm takes its name from cofounder Diane Szukovathy's 1990s art installation, which covered a Seattle building with four hundred copper-colored Jell-O molds, earning the grunge-era destination a cult fan base. Today, similarly quirky decor appears at the flower farm she and her musician husband, Dennis Westphall, operate in Washington's Skagit Valley, where shiny Jell-O molds dot the facades of outbuildings and spiral around a telephone pole to help visitors know they've arrived at the right place.

Diane and Dennis once supported themselves as landscapers. In 2001, their desire to find land that could provide their livelihoods brought them from the city to the country, where they found a small farmhouse surrounded by just over seven acres in Mount Vernon, Washington, an agricultural region home to some of the largest tulip bulb farms in the country and known for its famed Skagit Valley Tulip Festival.

The couple began as food farmers, planting a big orchard, berry crops, and vegetables. "We found out very quickly that there's no way we could pay the bills selling at farmers' markets," Dennis recalls. They did, however, discover that florists wanted to buy branches and foliage from their ornamental plants, including the fruit trees. With the addition of many other crops, including annual flowers and dahlias, Diane and Dennis developed a weekly delivery route to serve a network of Seattle flower shops. They loved wowing florists with Jello Mold's unique botanicals, but found this business model was limited because the route only served ten to twelve clients on a single day. Their landscaping work continued to subsidize the flower sales, and they wanted more stability for the business. "We approached this problem like creatives would," Diane recalls. "We had this mission of wanting to live on our own piece of land. But we had to figure out how to make a living from it in order to stay here."

In 2010, their community-building roots provided an inspiring solution as Diane and Dennis, along with fifteen other Washingtonian, Oregonian, and Alaskan flower farmers, established the Seattle Wholesale Growers Market, a producers' cooperative, to sell flowers through a small Seattle warehouse. Through the scrappy enterprise, Jello Mold has developed a reputation for its experimental farming approach, introducing uncommon plants to the marketplace, including winter-blooming hellebores and foliage crops. Jello Mold's foliage display is affectionately called the "salad bar" for its diversity.

Opposite: Dennis Westphall and Diane Szukovathy founded Jello Mold Farm in 2001, when they pursued a dream of building a land-based lifestyle and began growing cut flowers for the Seattle floral marketplace. Both are also artists and advocates for sustainably grown flowers and view farming as a vehicle for building community.

JELLOMOLDFARM.COM | @JELLOMOLDFARM

Diane and Dennis's ability to notice a plant's potential is best illustrated by the story of the snowberry foliage. "We grew Hancock snowberry [*Symphoricarpos × chenaultii* 'Hancock'] to pick before Thanksgiving and Christmas, sold for its cranberry-colored berries," Diane explains. "But that's a narrow window, and we needed a prolific crop to sell in the summer months, when our customers were spending much more on local flowers and foliage." Dennis thought Hancock snowberry's velvety foliage had potential, so he cut some branches in early summer (long before its berries are produced), and took sample bunches to the Market, handing them out like party favors. "It turned out to be one of the best foliage crops around. It's invincible," he says. Surprising designers with something new is part of the thrill that motivates these farmers. "They are the beautiful people who decide they're going to buy local flowers and support our business. We've created an incredible community of real relationships. It's kind of magical, but everyone has a role and that's how community works," Diane adds.

Dennis is known as the "mayor" of the Market, and after more than a dozen years bringing vibrant flowers to Seattle each week, he knows almost every florist, including their spouse's and kids' names. He maintains a closet filled with vintage Hawaiian shirts, a wardrobe that feels in sync with the Jello Mold brand when he dons a different one each week. "Most farmers are introverts," Diane maintains. "But one of the ways to keep Dennis happy on the farm

At left from top: Counting stems for a bunch of just-harvested scabiosa, a stunning variety called 'Black Knight'. Meghan Ellsworth is a member of Jello Mold's informal mentoring program, in which farmers spend part of each week at Jello Mol. *Opposite*: The iconic, two-story red barn stands tall along the central pathway. It is topped by a quirky cupola that can be seen for miles. The lower level stores farm equipment and is home to the flower-processing studio.

is that he can go see hundreds of his best friends at the Market every Wednesday. It's heartfelt watching him connect with florists."

Growing flowers is one thing, but growing farmers is equally part of Jello Mold's mission. Through nearly fifteen years as Market members, Diane and Dennis, along with other farmers, have invested in the future of floral agriculture by mentoring and educating new growers, especially women farmers. Several of the current Market members were once Jello Mold Farm interns or crew, and Diane and Dennis also operate an informal farmer incubation program, as three emerging growers spend part of each week farming alongside them. The couple wants to change the economics of flower farming so that families can sustain themselves and farms can be viable rather than just a side hustle, Diane explains. "The effort I put into the Market is to leave behind the chance for other people to peacefully raise their families doing what we've also done—growing and selling flowers."

Diane and Dennis are futurists, and in recent years, they have reshaped Jello Mold Farm to provide a more balanced lifestyle. There are still the busy weeks between April and October when Dennis wakes up at 3 A.M. to drive the truck sixty-five miles south to Seattle in order to get Jello Mold's buckets of branches, flowers, and foliage to the Market floor before doors open to shoppers at 6 A.M. But that grind has been offset by a radical choice in 2022, when he and Diane decided to eliminate dahlias from their crop mix, inviting area growers to dig up thousands of Jello Mold's dahlia tubers for new homes on neighboring farms. "We dropped some really intensive crops, but we're still growing a good range of plants—mostly trees and shrubs," Dennis notes. "What's different is that for the first time in twelve years, we now have two days off each week and we feel like we've achieved a work-life balance that may keep us farming for another ten or fifteen years—because that's going to keep us younger!"

Opposite: When crops need to be harvested in small batches, a low-tech wagon does the job. *Above*: A quiet moment in the doorway of a high tunnel. These structures are important for helping with season extension, which provides extra protection from the elements and coaxes flowers into bloom early in the season or late into fall.

HELLEBORE

Helleborus orientalis, Helleborus × hybridus,
species and cultivars
(common names, Christmas rose and Lenten rose)

12"–36"
Part Sun or Shade
Drought tolerant
   (low to moderate water needs)
Perennial

FAVORITE VARIETIES

For outdoor growing: *Helleborus orientalis* and hybrids,
   including all of the Wedding Party (single blooms)
   and Honeymoon series (double blooms), especially
   'Dark and Handsome', 'New York Night', 'Romantic
   Getaway', 'Tropical Sunset', 'French Kiss', and
   'Blushing Bridesmaid'
For hoop house growing: HGC Ice N' Roses series
   ('Red,' 'White,' 'Bianco,' 'Picotee,' 'Barolo' and 'Rose'),
   FrostKiss series 'Cheryl's Shine'

The star of winter cut flowers, hellebores kick off the local floral season in many regions around the globe, but they are particularly successful in the Pacific Northwest's landscapes. The name "hellebore" is thought to originate from the Greek name for *Helleborus orientalis*: *helleboros*, from root words meaning "to injure" and "food," a reference to the toxic attributes of the plant and its roots.

   With intriguing flower shapes (including double and picotee forms), petal palettes that range from creamy white and pale celadon to dark burgundy–black, and beautiful, leathery green foliage, the hellebore's original popularity began in the garden. That's where Diane and Dennis first encountered the winter-blooming perennial, which was uniquely suited for their clients' woodland landscapes when they worked as estate gardeners. Hellebore blooms can last for a few months in the landscape, but when grown as cut flowers, specific steps must be taken to ensure several days' of successful vase life—methods

Below: Helleborus HGC Ice N' Roses 'Red'.

262

Above: Helleborus HGC Ice N' Roses 'Rosado'.

that Jello Mold Farm has tested for years to improve the flower's performance for florists' needs.

Diane and Dennis have raised hundreds of *H. orientalis* plants in beds and borders under the high-branched trees that line their property. The perennials often seed themselves, producing more plants. But with climate change, there has been a risk that late winter snowstorms and freezes can damage these crops, so the couple began to research potential varieties to grow under cover, in two of Jello Mold's high tunnels.

Through a sales rep for a German hellebore breeder, Diane and Dennis learned about some of the species' newer hybrids, and they began to test introductions like Icc N' Roses 'Red' and FrostKiss 'Cheryl's Shine'. "These plants were originally hybridized for the European market, because Europeans use hellebores similarly to how we use poinsettias as a holiday plant in the US," Diane explains. The hybrids have been bred to produce large flowers that face outward (rather than downward), supported by tall, upright stems—just what florists want, she notes. "We dedicated two hoop

houses to hellebores and planted hundreds of plugs of them. By the following year, we took a truckload of hellebore bunches into the Market for Valentine's Day."

In a marketplace with customers who care about sourcing locally grown flowers, most florists have struggled to find a beautiful alternative to imported red roses at Valentine's Day, so these Jello Mold–grown hellebores are filling an important seasonal role, the growers note.

WHEN TO PLANT
This perennial can be planted in fall or spring. Can be grown in Zones 3 to 8.

WHERE TO BUY
Most specialty garden centers and nurseries stock perennial hellebore plants. Mail-order sources:
   Bluestone Perennials, bluestoneperennials.com
   Wayside Gardens, waysidegardens.com

HOW TO WATER
Water regularly until the hellebore plants are established. Unless there is an extended dry period, you won't need to provide additional irrigation.

WHEN TO HARVEST
Helleborus orientalis: Harvest stems once the first and second flowers bloom completely and drop the stamens, so that seed pods have begun to form in the flowers' centers. If you harvest any earlier, the cut flowers may droop very quickly.

   Hybrid hellebores (Ice N' Roses and FrostKiss series): Harvest stems once the second flower has started to open.

the FLOWER INDEX

ANEMONE *p. 140*
10"–12"
Full Sun to Part Shade
Prefers well-drained, moist soil
and cool temperatures
Corm grown as an annual or perennial

ASTILBE *p. 246*
24"–30"
Part Shade to Full Shade
Perennial

DELPHINIUM *p. 150*
36"–48"
Full Sun to Light Shade
Prefers rich, well-drained soil
Perennial

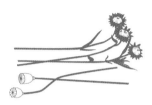

DRIED FLOWERS *p. 208*
Amaranth, Ammobium,
Celosia, Larkspur, Lepidium,
Nigella, *Setaria viridis*
(or any grasses or grains), Statice,
Shirley poppy, Strawflower

FLOWERING BRANCHES *p. 106*
Abelia, Flowering fruit trees
(apple, cherry, peach), Forsythia,
Mock orange, Quince, Spiraea,
Viburnum, Weigela
Woody shrubs

FLOWERING TOBACCO *p. 60*
18"–38"
Light Shade to Full Sun (prefers shade
from hot afternoon sun)
Perennial

HERBS *p. 68*
Ornamental basil (A), Bouquet dill (A),
Feverfew (P), Lavender (P),
Lemon verbena (P), Mint (P),
Mountain mint (P), Oregano (P),
Sage (P), Yarrow (P)

LAVENDER *p. 190*
28"–40" tall × 2'–5' wide
Full Sun
Prefers well-drained soil but
tolerates poor soil
Woody shrub

LISIANTHUS *p. 26*
24"–36"
Full Sun
Prefers moist, loamy soil
Native perennial, grown as an annual

MARIGOLD *p. 116*
24"–36"
Full Sun
Prefers moist, loamy soil but is tolerant
of poor soil if consistently watered
Annual

SANGUISORBA *p. 182*
30"–36"
Part Shade to Full Sun
Prefers moderately fertile, moist,
well-drained soil
Perennial

SNAPDRAGON *p. 88*
18"–30"
Full Sun
Prefers fertile, sharply-drained soil
and cool temperatures
Perennial subshrub grown as an annual

SWEET WILLIAM *p. 226*
6"–24"
Full Sun to Part Shade
Rich, well-drained soil
Perennial or annual

TULIP *p. 254*
12"–30"
Full Sun
Moderate to regular water
Bulb grown as an annual

CELOSIA *p. 96*
12"–48"
Full Sun
Drought and heat tolerant (low to
moderate water needs)
Annual

CHRYSANTHEMUM *p. 240*
36"–40"
Full to Part Shade
Prefers a balanced mix of loamy soil
Perennial

CLEMATIS *p. 156*
Vines up to 6' or 8'
Shrub varieties up to 4'
Requires up to 6 hours full sun but
prefers shaded roots
Keep roots regularly watered
during the first two seasons until
plant is established
Woody vine

DAHLIA *p. 164*
24"–48"
Full Sun
Heat tolerant
Requires a consistent supply of water
in well-drained soil
Tuber grown as an annual or perennial

FOXGLOVE *p. 52*
36"
Full Sun to Part Shade
Tender perennial or biennial

GARDEN-GATHERED *p. 218*
Moss, Checkered lily, *Eucalyptus*,
Fatsia japonica, *Holboellia* spp.,
Lichen, Love-in-a-mist,
Orchids, Shield fern,
Twig dogwood

GOOSENECK LOOSESTRIFE *p. 44*
36"–40"
Full to Part Shade
Prefers moist soil; will tolerate dry
conditions in shade, but plants
will not flourish; vigorous spreader
Perennial

HELLEBORE *p. 262*
12"–36"
Part Sun or Shade
Drought tolerant (low to
moderate water needs)
Perennial

PEONY *p. 124*
24"–33"
Full Sun
Prefers fertile, well-drained soil but
can tolerate many types of soil
Perennial

POPPY *p. 80*
7"–16"
Full Sun
Moderate to regular water
Tender perennial grown as an annual

RANUNCULUS *p. 132*
12"–18"
Full to Part Sun
Prefers moist soil and cool temperatures
Herbaceous perennial grown as an annual

ROSE *p. 234*
3'–9' high × 3'–6' wide
Full to Part Sun
Consistent water required
Woody shrub

WINTERBERRY *p. 32*
12' tall × 12' wide
Full Sun
Prefers wet or moist soil
Woody shrub

YARROW *p. 198*
30"–36"
Full Sun
Drought and heat tolerant (low to
moderate water needs)
Native perennial

ZINNIA *p. 174*
12"–18"
Full Sun
Drought and heat tolerant (low to
moderate water needs)
Annual

(A) Annual   (P) Perennial

Floral Futures

The changing of the seasons grounds us in the present. The progression of the year's four seasons helps us relate to our environment in ways that can provide sustenance, beauty, and clues as to what might lie ahead. Seasonal flowers do this, too: They ground us in time and place. They provide a meaningful and ecologically relevant way to engage with our environment. Stated more simply: Flowers just make sense.

The stories and photos contained in these pages provide a beautiful illustration of the importance of seasonality and how flower farmers across North America are working hard to change our expectations of what is possible with locally grown, seasonal flowers. But more than that, these farmers are offering what feels like a magical bouquet of solutions to the pressing challenges posed by climate change. As the world grapples with the escalating impacts of global warming, decreased biodiversity, and pollution, it is the growing number of small-scale, local flower farmers who are emerging as a beacon of hope, offering meaningful benefits for both the environment and communities.

At its core, local flower farming embodies the principles of sustainability and environmental stewardship. By cultivating flowers close to their point of consumption, farmers minimize the carbon footprint associated with transportation. They also promote biodiversity and conservation efforts by cultivating a variety of flower species suited to local climates and soil conditions. They act as literal on-the-ground agents of change, helping to support a sustainable future that includes all of the beauty that is possible with locally grown flowers.

The most frequently quoted definition of sustainability comes from the UN World Commission on Environment and Development and the 1987 Brundtland Commission Report: "Sustainable development is development that meets the needs of the present without compromising the ability of future generations to meet their own needs." This means thinking outside of ourselves and working in a way that protects the environment and society to ensure our children (and their children) can inherit a healthy Earth. It also means understanding that the future will be what we make of it right now.

I often think of sustainability as something along the lines of a patchwork quilt: pieces of fabric that are sewn together in a way that makes the sum of the parts greater than the whole. Excluding some pieces means that there are holes. Not using thread to sew together all the pieces? You have nothing but unusable scraps. The golden thread that keeps the pieces together and is ultimately what makes sustainability work? Community.

As I have studied sustainability at Harvard University over the past several years—and as I currently write my thesis on the environmental and social life cycle of roses grown in North America—I have been reminded of the fragility of not only our planet, but of our egos. Change feels hard. And hard work is daunting. Let the stories of these flower farmers remind us of the value of hard work and how small actions can lead to sweeping change.

As consumers increasingly prioritize ethical and environmentally conscious choices, supporting local flower farming emerges as a tangible way to mitigate climate change while nurturing vibrant and resilient communities. As Rebecca Solnit stated so beautifully in *Orwell's Roses*, "A flower is a node on a network of botanical systems of interconnection and regeneration." It is indeed this kind of interconnection and regeneration that makes the Slow Flowers movement so powerful and so desperately needed during this intense period of climate change. So, celebrate your local flower farmers. Buy from them. Enjoy seasonal flowers. Your brains will thank you. And so will the planet.

—Becky Feasby
Prairie Girl Flowers
Calgary, Alberta, Canada

Acknowledgments

A bouquet of thanks.

We must begin by thanking each of the flower farmers who shared their stories and every one of the photographers whose work is highlighted in this beautiful book. Your expressions of flower farming are true magic!

We sit in awe of the grit and grace reflected by each farm's narrative. There are twenty-nine farms featured, hailing from across North America. We are inspired by the families, generations, loves, losses, hopes, and dreams of each one who planted a seed and nurtured a flower into a vibrant economic enterprise.

We are so appreciative of our editor, Shawna Mullen, and the talented team at Abrams, including Emily Wardwell, whose beautiful design work brought each farmer's story to life. Thanks, also, to Jenice Kim, design manager; Logan Hill and Annalea Manalili, managing editors; Hannah Braden, editorial assistant, and Kathleen Gaffney, production manager. We are grateful for Daniel Sparler's careful editing of botanical Latin plant names throughout the book.

A very special thank you to our friend Mary Grace Long, whose cover photography depicts Jello Mold Farm's sparkling pink hellebores, held by Meghan Ellsworth, a young farmer mentored by flower farmers Diane Szukovathy and Dennis Westphall (p. 256). We love this image, and we are thrilled that it communicates the creative spirit of *The Flower Farmers*.

We're so grateful that you've picked up this book. As you spend time with it, we hope you gain new appreciation for flower farmers, their hard work, passion, and dedication. These profiles will introduce you to the people behind the flowers; the accompanying botanical profiles introduce you to crops you can plant in your own garden patch. Enjoy!

Opposite: A gathering of Everyday Flowers' romantic anemones, in a mix called 'Galilee Pastel', which produces cream, light pink, and light purple blooms—each with a contrasting dark center.

About the Authors

As personal and professional friends, Robin and Debra have enjoyed collaborating since 2009, when they met on a press tour at the Northwest Flower & Garden Show. Lunch soon followed, and Robin invited Debra to join a group of writers to produce a lifestyle insights blog, social media channel, and trend analysis consultancy (that turned out to be just a little ahead of its time—but a perfect fit for Robin's years of consumer research and Debra's experience as a garden and lifestyle journalist). This collaboration yielded a desire to continue working together, and that wish came true several years later, when the pair produced *Slow Flowers Journal*, vol. 1 for Wildflower Media (one of nearly a dozen books that Robin produced as its book editor). In 2020, Debra and Robin combined forces to launch BLOOM Imprint LLC, where they produce books by and about flower farmers, floral designers, and creatives in the Slow Flowers movement (including Debra's book *Where We Bloom*.)

DEBRA PRINZING is the author of twelve books and the founder and producer of SlowFlowers.com, the online directory of American and Canadian flower farms, florists, shops, and studios that supply domestic and local flowers. In 2015, she founded American Flowers Week, which occurs annually in late June. For the past seven years she has produced the annual Slow Flowers Summit, dubbed the TED Talk for floral professionals.

ROBIN AVNI is a creative director and experienced designer in the media and high-tech industries. Her specialties include creative management of award-winning teams and content development. She has produced eighteen floral and lifestyle books, including eight in collaboration with *The Flower Farmers* coauthor Debra Prinzing, showcasing the floral lifestyle of creatives and entrepreneurs.

Opposite: Poppies in bud, from 3 Porch Farm.
At left: Authors, from top: Debra Prinzing and Robin Avni

Photography Credits

Chasers of the Light Photography: pages 2, 142 (top middle), 145–151; Missy Palacol Photography: pages 4, 201 (top), 222–227, 234, 238, 241, 249, 251-252, 268, 271 (top); Fennel Harper: pages 6, 14, 55–59; Anna-Alexia Basile: page 9; Daniel Dent: pages 11, 71 (lower right), 73–81, 272; Ana Gambuto: pages 13, 14 (upper left), 17, 18 (lower left), 19, 20 (upper left, bottom), 22–26; Elisabeth Waller Photography: pages 14, 35, 36 (upper right, bottom), 38, 43, 45; Peta Marie Sommers: pages 14 (lower left), 47–50; Beth Caldwell Photography: pages 15 (lower right), 29–33; Jordan Veitinger: pages 15 (top), 63, 67; Hans Li: pages: 18 (upper left), 20 (upper right); Abby Matson: pages 36 (upper left), 39, 42, 44; Lisa Cassell-Arms: page 40; Johnny's Seeds: pages 52–53; The Floral Society: page 60; Katie Tolson: page 61; Xenia D'Ambrosi: pages 64–65, 68–69; Elizabeth Seliga/3 Cats Photo: pages 70 (lower left), 99–107; Jessica Adaway: pages 70 (upper left), 83–89; Sebastian Tongson Jr.: pages 71, 91–97; Kim Dillon: pages 108 (upper right, bottom middle), 137, 138; Lindsey McCullough and Mindy Carter of Red Twig Farms: pages 108 (lower left), 119–125; Jules Regalado: pages 109 (top), 113, 114 (upper right); Owl & Key: pages 109 (bottom), 131; Sierra Pries: pages 111, 114, 116–117; Crystal Salkeld: page 114 (bottom); Maria Lourdes Casañares-Still: page 114 (upper left); James Janeri: pages 127, 128 (lower right); Gretel Adams: pages 128 (upper left, upper right, lower left), 130, 132, 133; Carmen Troesser: pages 135, 139–141; Amber Lanphier: pages 142, 159–160, 162 (upper right), 163 (top), 165; Bonnie Sen: pages 142 (center), 194–195, 197 (bottom), 198–199; Elizabeth Lanier Photography: pages 142 (lower left), 179 (bottom), 181; Ngoc Minh Ngo: pages 142, 153–154; Ashley Marie Photography: pages 143 (upper right), 185, 189 (top); Pomaikai Photo: page 143; Caitlin Atkinson: pages 155–157; Sydney Carle: pages 162 (bottom), 163 (bottom left and bottom right), 164; Allison Keener: page 162 (upper left); Lehua Moon Photography: pages 167, 171, 173 (top and bottom); Christian Ingalls: pages 168–169, 172, 174–175; Keeley McKay Photography: page 177; Orange Photographie: pages 178, 179 (top); Julio Freitas: pages 180, 182, 183; Hansen Film Company: pages 186, 187 (bottom); Southwest Creative Company: page 187 (top); Wonder Media: pages 188, 189 (bottom); Calhoun Flower Farms: pages 190, 191; Brianna Bosch: pages 193, 197 (top and bottom left); Amber Fouts: pages 200 (upper left, top center), 201 (middle right), 211–217, 220, 237, 240, 241 (left); Emma May Lowery: pages 200 (center), 228–233; Krista Rossow: pages 200 (lower left), 202–209; Lia Crowe: pages 200 (bottom right), 243, 245; Mary Grace Long: pages 201, 256–263; Rizaniño Reyes: pages 218–219; Yumi Nagumo: pages 244, 246, 247 (top); Julie Remy: page 247; Tracy Yang: pages 250, 254; Nikki Collette: page 267; Heather Marino: page 271 (right)

Editor: Shawna Mullen
Designer: Emily Wardwell
Design Manager: Jenice Kim
Managing Editors: Logan Hill and Annalea Manalili
Production Manager: Kathleen Gaffney
Horticulture Consultant: Daniel Sparler

Library of Congress Control Number: 2024942495

ISBN: 978-1-4197-7569-7
eISBN: 979-8-88707-348-4

Printed and bound in China
10 9 8 7 6 5 4 3 2 1

Abrams books are available at special discounts when
purchased in quantity for premiums and promotions as
well as fundraising or educational use. Special editions
can also be created to specification. For details, contact
specialsales@abramsbooks.com or the address below.

Abrams® is a registered trademark of Harry N. Abrams, Inc.

ABRAMS The Art of Books
195 Broadway, New York, NY 10007
abramsbooks.com